Talking with Children

TALKING WITH CHILDREN

RONALD F. REED

ARDEN PRESS, INC.

Denver, Colorado

Library of Congress Cataloging in Publication Data

Reed, Ronald F.
    Talking with children.

    1. Parent and child.   2. Conversation.   3. School
environment.   I. Title.
HQ755.85.R43   1983   158'.24   83-9990
ISBN 0-912869-00-3
        0-912869-01-1 (pbk.)

Published in the United States of America
Arden Press, Inc.
Denver, Colorado

To Ann

TABLE
OF
CONTENTS

PREFACE

When you look at the literature you find that very little has been written about parent-child talk, though a great deal of work has been done on teacher-student talk. This book attempts to build some bridges for those who believe it is the job of *both* the school and the home to help young children make sense of their environments and to deal with all that happens to them. The world as it is presented to us needs interpretation; individual parts do not come with neat labels attached. (That is why it is so easy to lie to small children and why the humor of tall tales is often lost on them—they have few experiences with which to contrast the tall tale; the tall tale does not conflict with anything.) It is our responsibility as parents to give them the tools of interpretation. But this is not a matter of indoctrination, of simply providing the labels; rather, our responsibility is to help our children to build, evaluate, and adapt their own interpretive schemes. We do this by talking with them, by allowing them to raise questions, by walking with them toward answers, by revealing to them that we have questions, too.

Now, some talks are better than others. Each chapter of *Talking with Children* has focused on an individual aspect of the parent-child talking relationship in order that we might become aware of all that is involved in a successful parent-child conversation. The book begins with a discussion of the power of talk, the effects successful talking can have upon the individual *and* the community. It then approaches who our children are. No attempt is made here to list characteristics that all children share; rather, only those characteristics are discussed that are typical of children in general and that should be kept in mind when we find ourselves involved in the often rewarding, often frustrating activity of talking with our children. Given these typical characteristics, we can formulate rules and suggestions meant to facilitate conversations that lie within the different types of talk discussed in the fourth and fifth chapters of the book. These suggestions will help maintain your talking relationship and should help you to avoid those moments when talk breaks down. Conversations with children dissolve for recognizable reasons, and a chapter of this book is devoted to resolving those problems. Finally, since the talk that adults have with children does not exist in a vacuum, some space is given here to the relationships of other people, of schools, and of developmental psychology to the parent-child talking relationship.

A word of caution. Children, like adults, need variety. Nobody sits around all day trying to make sense of his or her experience. Children joke, giggle, squirm, and fidget. They don't *always* want to reflect on their experience or to talk with you about it, and they shouldn't have to. They should be free to be childish. Part and only part of childhood involves the attempt to make sense of things. In this book I will deal with that part. It would be a mistake to assume, say, that the abilities to make scary faces or to swallow and hum at the same time were being denigrated. They are not. I just do not talk about them here.

Some of the most significant work in the field of adult-child relations has been done by Professor Matthew Lipman of the Institute for the Advancement of Philosophy for Children. I was fortunate to receive some training at the Institute, and this book, in part, represents my attempt to utilize some of the principles of the Philosophy for Children program outside of the classroom environment. Professor Lipman has influenced my thinking, and I owe him a great deal. All writers need an intellectual conscience. He stood as mine. Still, I am the one responsible for this book.

I received a great deal of encouragement and support during the writing of this book. Indeed, I spent years just listening to conversations, trying to find out what makes a conversation "work." I cannot thank all of those people individually. Let this stand as my note of thanks to them.

The administrators, in particular the president, of Texas Wesleyan College, Jon H. Fleming, have encouraged me financially and emotionally. Without both kinds of support this book would never have been written.

I received financial support from the Sid Richardson Foundation and the Sam Taylor Foundation. Their support gave me the time and the means to travel to libraries around the country to do research on this book.

I tried out a number of ideas on colleagues and graduate students, in particular Ron Rembert and Caroline Nickel. The book is better for their comments and criticism.

Special thanks to Frederick Ramey, my editor, and Ann Margaret Sharp of the Institute for the Advancement of Philosophy for Children. Both made almost innumerable suggestions. Invariably, those suggestions were helpful and to the point. Alas, they should not be blamed for any weakness in the book. That, as they say, is my responsibility.

Writing this book turned into more than an academic enterprise for me. When things got particularly difficult, Joe Mitchell of Texas Wesleyan always offered friendship and sound advice.

Thanks to my family. I miss talking to my mother and father. While writing the conversations in this book I could almost hear their voices.

Adam, Jeremy, and Rebecca, my children, have been wonderful before, during and after (I hope) the writing of this book. They are very nice kids.

Finally, thanks to Ann. This book is for her.

THE IMPORTANCE OF TALKING

We spend a lot of time talking. It seems that people are always talking and that nothing ever gets done. In large part, we move from platitude to platitude. We say that talk is cheap, and we believe that all the time we spend talking has been wasted if the talk does not lead to some kind of action, if we do not learn something, if, in fact, the talk does not produce something.

Children between the ages of five and sixteen spend 15,000 hours in the classroom and 45,000 hours in front of the television, and in both of these situations they are relatively passive spectators. Children also spend a good deal of time sleeping. Clearly, they do not have much time for talking with adults. Moreover, when we add all of the preceding to the fact that children and adults occupy largely different worlds—the child exists in the playground and the schoolroom, the adult in the factory and the office—it becomes extremely difficult to accept the platitude in any of its forms but especially as it relates to the talk between adults and children. Talk between an adult and a child is precious if only because of its rarity in comparison with the other activities that children and adults perform.

That is not the only reason talking is precious. It is also precious because of its very power. Let us say that talk is powerful in the following ways: cognitively, affectively, politically, and, coining a rather barbaric term, "definitionally."

When we talk with somebody else, there can be a cognitive exchange. After I talk with you, I may walk away from the conversation in better cognitive shape than when I walked in. I can learn something from you. I can understand more, see more connections, figure out how to do something. You, in turn, might pick up some information from me. Your ability to deal with the world might improve as the result of our conversation. Thus, sometimes when we talk, one of us receives what we might call a cognitive benefit. At other times we both benefit. At still other times the cognitive aspect is missing altogether. We do not always talk in order to swap information. Sometimes we talk simply "to pass the time away." Finally, there are times when talk has what we might call a cognitive harm. You and I get together and we swap *misinformation.* Either or both of us come away in worse cognitive shape than when we entered the conversation. Talk, then, can affect cognitive ability, but we need to recognize that this is not the sole purpose of talking, nor is it the most important aspect of talking. Especially as talking takes place between child and adult, it need not have a cognitive aspect to be considered worthwhile. The child does not *always* have to learn a lesson when she talks to the adult.

When we speak about the affective aspect of talking we are forced to speak figuratively. We do not have, our language does not have, a nice, precise way of dealing with emotions. Still, we all know what it means to feel warm or cool toward someone. Also, we all know that it is possible to express that emotion and, sometimes, even to create that emotion by a look, by a touch, by a caress. William James said that sometimes we cry because we are sad, but other times we are sad because we cry.

We can achieve that same end by talking. The very physical act of one person talking with another person can create a bond, can strengthen an already existing bond, or destroy it. We utter the platitude that talk is cheap and then we realize that talk often significantly affects what people know, do, and feel. It becomes difficult, at this point, to think of anything *more* valuable than talk.

The political power of talk is its effectiveness in building what John Dewey called "like-mindedness." It is possible to imagine a society in which all communication is done by letter—a community that has, we might expect, much lower postal rates than our own. However, when we look at our community and at other communities, we see that they comprise a set of people sharing the same fundamental sets of beliefs, values, hopes, ideals, and aspirations. This is not to say that communities do not grow, but only that if this group is a community, and not just an aggregate of people, there has to be some form of like-mindedness. Now, the way that we, in fact, build community is quite different from the way our letter-writing friends might attempt to build a community. (Indeed, it is hard for me to imagine how they would go about building a community.) We form communities over extended periods of time. People have to get to know each other before communities are formed or before they can gain access to an existing community. They literally have to sit down and talk it over.

The town meetings in New England are prime examples of this (although at some of the meetings there is more standing up and shouting than sitting down and talking). The town meeting is not simply a raising of the "voice" of the community. In some sense, the talking that people do at town meetings differentiates one town from another and differentiates the class of towns that have meetings from the class of towns that do not. But even when we do not have town meetings, the way we talk about things is one important way to discover or build like-mindedness, to discover or build communities. Take talking away from people and they will quickly have to discover a substitute for talking, or they will stop living in communities. This is one reason the education of the deaf is so important for members of the community who are *not* deaf. The deaf are precluded from the ready interchange that we call "talking." They are blocked from using the "key" that most of us use to gain admittance to the larger society. Unless they can discover a substitute key (sign language), they will be denied admission to the larger community. Besides the obvious moral reasons for not overtly or covertly denying membership to the community because of something like hearing impairment, there are equally as obvious practical reasons (there are many deaf people, there are many untapped potentials and resources, etc.). Simply, if people cannot talk, the community has an obligation to ensure its own health by establishing a substitute for talking.

Finally, how we talk about things, in large part, determines how we relate to our environment. It determines our characteristic attitudes toward the world. Our talk goes a long way toward fixing our identity as groups and as individuals; this is its "definitional" power. I label this thing as "good," and I go out of my way to achieve it because it is said to be good. We say that this is a good car; we want good cars; therefore, we want this car. We say, on the other hand, that this activity is a bad one and that anyone who performs that activity is guilty. If we could say that the activity (the same activity) was a good one, we might give that person a decoration or a commendation. In one case, we behold the murderer; in the other case, we discover the war hero.

Moreover, without getting into a debate on, say, Black English *versus* Standard English, it is apparent that if a teacher compels a child to talk, invariably, in a single dialect, he significantly limits the child's ability to relate to various social groups. If, for example, the teacher tells a child that the way he speaks is "wrong," and if the child believes him, and if all the significant adults in the child's nonschool environment speak that way, then, the child has been introduced to a powerful dilemma. If he talks to those adults in the way the teacher counsels, he will no longer "fit in" as he once did. He will become, in effect, a different character to that group. If, on the other hand, he talks in school as they talk he will probably be labeled as "recalcitrant" or "slow." How the child talks bears directly on the perception of his character. He goes from being thin-Eugene-who-lives-in-an-apartment-on-Sterling-St.-with-his-parents-and-three-sisters to thin-Eugene-who-lives-in-an-apartment-on-Sterling St.-with-his-parents-and-three-sisters-and-is-also-a-slow-learner. Eugene, if he is smart, will quickly learn that it is to his benefit to speak one way at home and one way in the school. At home, he will talk the way he always has and will continue to fit in with his friends and family. At school, he will talk the way the teacher says he should. He will speak Standard English and be labeled a good student. Eugene will also learn that the school and the rest of the world exist on completely different planes and that what happens in one place has very little effect on what happens in the other. But that, sad as it is, is a problem we need not deal with here.

I have said that talking is precious because it can effect a cognitive and affective change, because it is an effective tool for building a community, and because it goes a long way toward defining what constitutes the individual and how the individual is related to other individuals. And given the rarity of talk between adults and children, you might be feeling some trepidation, some apprehension as a talking parent. It would be a mistake if you felt so much apprehension that you could not speak to your child. (Your child, if he is anything like most children, and you, if you are anything like most parents, would not put up with that apprehension for long. No matter what your apprehension, you will be talking with your child before, during, and after you read this or any other book.) Still, a little apprehension can be a good thing if it causes you to value every conversation you have with your child. Think, for a moment, of the teacher who is preparing a lecture for her class. She does not know *exactly* what she will say. She knows where she wants to go with her talk, but she is not going to read a speech. The words that she will utter and the combinations in which those words will be placed are, in a very real sense, "open." The teacher, and let us assume that she is a good one, often does not know what she will say until she sees what the preceding words lead to. (Catch a good teacher with her guard down and after a particularly good class, and she may admit that she said things that she did not even know that she knew. She may learn as much from the lecture as her students.) She also, and this is a crucial point, does not know which questions, or even what sorts of questions the students will ask. She has to be prepared to respond to those questions and to weave her answers into her "prepared" talk. If she does not do this, she will wind up with a talk that has no direct relationship to the questions or the interests of her students. The teacher has some grounds for feeling anxious.

Admittedly, the teacher has a good amount of control over her talk; she has a specific subject matter. She can legitimately say that noun-verb agreement is irrelevant to the historical process and that "If you want to talk about noun-verb agreement you should go see a grammarian." The teacher has certain office hours. The teacher can go home. The parent lives in a much less tidy universe. Even granting all of this, however, some similarities obtain between teacher-student talk and some parent-child talk. Sometimes when a child talks to his parents, he wants to learn something. In those cases the parent must have some relationship to the subject matter. This is not to say that the parent has to be an expert in all areas, but only that the parent must have some sort of *access to experts*. She must be able to come up with a way of helping the child discover new facts, to find out what, say, the most recent development in bio-engineering is. The parent must also have some *method* of helping the child to learn. Should the parent tell the answer or lead the child to the answer? What is the best method for helping the child learn something within the context of parent-child talk? And finally, the parent must have a very good idea as to what her child is like and what, in general, children are like. It is a mistake, a mistake we all are guilty of, to assume that our listeners are much like we are and that they therefore get the same "message" from a conversation that we get. The mistake may be and often is fatal to parent-child talk.

In later chapters, we will spend time dealing with the sort of parent-child talk that is a result of the child's wanting to know something. We will also deal with the forms of parent-child talk that are most emphatically not a result of the child's wanting to know something. (Remember, not all talk is meant to or must yield a cognitive gain.) But before doing that, we should spend some time talking about the types of people parents talk to when they talk to children. Kids are people, too. But they are special kinds of people.

SOME CHARACTERISTICS OF CHILDREN

How you view your child determines, in large part, how you will treat her. And what you will expect from her. And when you will be disappointed in her. And when you will beam over one of her accomplishments. And so on.

Traditionally, there have been two ways—these are not the only ones, but, historically, they are important—of looking at the child. The first tradition sees the child as a basically unruly creature who will do the wrong, the silly and the dangerous when confronted with a set of alternatives. The child in this view is, as it were, the personal equivalent of Murphy's law—if it can go wrong, the child will see to it that it does. The purpose of education is, in effect, to tame this wild animal. This is a tradition that many educators feel quite comfortable with. Education becomes a process of imposing a stronger will on a weaker one—for the benefit of the child, of course.

The second tradition sees the child as a basically healthy, moral creature who, if society and educators will just give her some room, will develop into a fine, productive member of society. If the first tradition counsels parents and educators to step in and control and combat the dangerous forces at work, the second counsels us to allow those forces to thrive. Oversimplified, the first tradition tells us to be afraid of the child, i.e., to control her impulses as quickly and efficiently as we can. The second tradition tells us to be afraid *for* the child, i.e., to control her environment so that it does not infringe on the child. The first tradition we usually call "authoritarian." The second is labeled "permissive."

Now, what is so curious about each of these viewpoints is that neither squares with the view that the observer would have if he spent some time simply watching children. Children are not always the enemy (although sometimes they can be a real nuisance). Their impulses are not always dangerous. Adults don't always have to control children. The world does not end if the child occasionally gets his way. Parents, especially working parents, find out quite soon that sometimes when you leave children alone they play together, are considerate, and are capable of real friendship and generosity.

But those *other* times when you leave the children alone make it quite difficult to accept what we have called the permissive view. In an earlier age, we would be tempted to call their behavior, at times, "demonic." We no longer use that kind of language—or we no longer admit to using that kind of language. Still, our experience with children gives us little reason to believe that children always know what is best for them or that we should simply allow the child to do that which he wills.

The nice part about the traditions we have referred to is that they enable parents and teachers to *do* something. Each has a view of the child's nature and each acts according to that view. The authoritarian teacher, for example, "does not smile until January," following an old educational maxim that is easy to follow if you don't have a sense of humor. Many nice and funny things happen in the classroom, and some of them happen before January. She asserts herself as authority in a given domain—the classroom. Students must and do, if she is effective, look to her for direction. The permissive teacher's view of the child enables her to *do* things as well. The locus of authority shifts from the teacher to the students and the students' interests and desires determine what is valuable and what should be done. The teacher simply reacts to those desires and interests.

Now, it is easy to reject both traditions; to repeat, neither view seems to square with the way children really are. When we reject each tradition, however, we are in the uncomfortable position of believing that we are right and still not knowing what we should *do*. Keep in mind that education is a sort of activity. It is something the more educated do with the less educated. In this case, it is something that parents and teachers do with children.

We need a plan of action, a strategy if you will. The strategy should be flexible. It should allow for individual differences, for the odd case, and for the unexpected. In brief, it should be an effective strategy. It should be composed of a set of principles that enables us better to understand the behavior of children and better to predict what will work (be educative) and what will not. Now the question is the following: "How do we begin to build such a strategy? Where should we start?" Given what we know about the authoritarian and the permissive tradition, the answer seems obvious. We should begin to build from the "material" at hand. We should do precisely what the authoritarian tradition and the permissive tradition did not do. Simply, we should look at children and attempt to "derive" our strategies from that.

Before going on, a few digressions are in order. It seems obvious that if you want to be a good parent or educator then you have to know something about children. It may be obvious, but many parents and educators do not see it. If you assume that you know what children are really like, if you assume that you can give a neat capsule description of the difference between the adult and the child, then chances are you will be in the same position as those members of the authoritarian tradition and those of the permissive tradition. You will not have to study and learn about (and *from*, I might add) children; consequently, the chances of your missing the boat as far as your child or student is concerned will be high.

Now, what is the first thing we notice when we look at children? Not surprisingly (and this may make us more sympathetic to the authoritarian and the permissive traditions), the first thing we notice is that there are a lot of different children out there. We say that all children have a certain characteristic, and along comes Rosalie who obviously does not have that characteristic. About the only characteristic that all children share is their age, and recognition of that hardly enables us to *do* anything.

We should recognize, early on, that our statements about children will probably never be universal. If we do stumble on a proposition that is true of all children, it will probably be trivial (all children were born after a certain date). At best, our statements will be general; they will be true of *many* or *most* children. We should remember that even if we do come up with an adequate strategy for talking and thinking with children, that strategy may not work precisely because this child is different from the children on whom the strategy is based. Finally, we should realize that a complete list of all the charac- teristics of all children is neither necessary nor practical. You don't have to know *everything* about children or about a partic- ular child in order to be a good parent or a good teacher. As always, however, the more you do know, the better off you will be.

Children are inexperienced.   There are two sides to expe- rience. Dewey called them the active and passive sides. On the active side, children, by virtue of their age, have not had the opportunity to do many things. Imagine a universe in which families travel to a different country for each summer vaca- tion. The child who is ten would have gone to more countries than the child who is five. The simple fact of the ten-year-old's age gives her a distinct advantage over the five-year-old. On the passive side, the ten-year-old has had more things happen to her. Again, imagine that same family. Imagine that both children always get sick on the first day of their vacation. The ten-year-old will have five more unpleasant experiences than the five-year-old.

We should stop for a moment and make sure that we do not overstate the case. Children, even the youngest of children, do have a host of experiences. That is why, for example, doctors stress that health care for the baby begins at conception, and why many hospitals, doctors, and parents are concerned about the barrenness of the delivery room. Yet even when we realize all of that, it is still apparent that experience, active and pas- sive, increases with age.

None of the preceding is meant to be earth shattering. I am simply pointing to the obvious: children are, in general, less experienced than adults. A point that we will try to make later is that some of the difficulty we encounter when we try to talk and think with children may *not* be caused by the fact that children think differently from adults. That is, children may be capable of the same sorts of intellectual operations as adults. Even very young children may be capable of deductive and inductive moves. What may stop them from successfully making those moves is that children do not have the appropriate "starting points" for the reasoning process. If we reason from our experience and if experience is lacking, then the reasoning process will break down.

Children, in general, are less effective language users than adults. Children have to learn grammar. They have to memorize vocabulary words. Language skills are not inborn. People have to spend a good deal of time studying and practicing a language before they become fluent (or before they become what we call fluent).

Besides being less effective language users than adults, children often adopt different linguistic conventions from those that adults adopt. For example, have you ever asked a seven-year-old what she did today? Chances are you got one of two sorts of answers. The first would be the simple "nothing." You respond, let us say, with an exasperated "But I haven't seen you in ten hours. What did you do all that time?" Again, you receive as a reply, "Nothing." If the first sort of answer is frustrating because of the lack of information gained, the second sort of answer is frustrating because of the overload of information. You ask, "How did you like the movie?" In reply, you get a complete and meandering description of the plot, ruminations about the script ("Should the hero have driven the car into the desert? Shouldn't he have known the bad guys would be after him? Shouldn't he have been driving a Trans-Am and not a Volkswagen?"), a report on what your son had to eat, what his sister ate, and what she said when she spilled her soda, opinions on all the people around him, and finally, comparisons with every other movie he has seen since October of 1981.

Children's talk is, at times, very different from that of adults. This is a function, in part, of their unfamiliarity with the language. It is also a function, in part, of their having different linguistic values or different ideas about what is important about speech or what needs to be said. To assume that children think differently from adults because they talk differently is, of course, precipitous. To ignore the fact that children's talking styles are often quite different from those of adults is to minimize the chance of effective communication between adults and children.

Children tend to talk and think with their bodies more than adults do. It takes a great deal of sophistication (and a great deal of patience) simply to sit still and think about something. Watch a child when she tries to explain something. Chances are she will not simply look you in the eye and utter a set of words. She will look at your neck and then your foot and then the TV. She will get up and sit down and tip over her milk. What she will not do, usually, is sit still.

Watch a child when he is listening or when he is trying to understand something. Chances are he will not *look* the same way adults look when they are trying to understand something. Children often look like they are not paying attention when in fact they are. (Again, let us be careful that we do not get carried away here. Often, when children look like they are not paying attention they, in fact, are not.) Children fidget. One of the best things to come out of the Progressive Movement in education in the United States was the realization that it is impossible to circumscribe children's physical activities without having a harmful effect on their thinking abilities. Figuratively, we can say that children think with their bodies. To force a child to sit still serves the same sort of function as constantly correcting a child's grammar while he is trying to tell a story. The child may get the grammar right but there is an obvious cost. Both you and the child will lose interest in the story. Both you and the child will focus on mechanics and, somehow, the story will be lost. Moreover, chances are there will be little carry-over from the "lesson" you give the child to the next story he attempts to tell. Not only will you lose the story but the grammar lesson will probably prove ineffective.

In a similar way, when we expend our energies and the child's energies on controlling his physical movement, it is foolish to think that either we or the child will be able to concentrate on anything but the task at hand—making the child be still. Furthermore, as even the most authoritarian teacher knows, you cannot really control the child's physical movement. At best, like a river, it can be rechanneled. You can stop a child from acting in one way but you cannot, unless you are willing to do irreparable damage, stop him from acting in *some* way.

Throughout this book, I will underscore that we are limiting our discussion to characteristics that *most* children have. I have consciously shied away from trying to describe characteristics that might be said to be constitutive of the "nature" of children. If, however, there is one characteristic that comes close to being applicable to all children it is that they fidget. Failure to recognize this, it would seem, effectively limits, if it does not preclude altogether, the possibility of effective and interesting talk between adults and children.

Children have an ability, an ability that many adults wish they had, to stop thinking about a problem. Often children will stop, as it were, in mid-sequence, not bothering to finish one story before beginning another or losing interest in a conversation a good while before the adult thinks the conversation is over. (This characteristic, obviously, is not the exclusive property of children. Think of the number of times this has happened to you while having a conversation with an adult, the number of times you realized that the other person was thinking of things other than your speech.)

There are two points to keep in mind here. The first is that very few children seem to have the same kind of psychological relationships to problems that many adults do. Children seem to have an ability—or a liability, depending on how you look at it—to leave a problem when they lose interest in it, and they will often lose interest in a problem at precisely that moment when an adult becomes most interested. This can be unsettling.

The second point to keep in mind is that the notion of "proper sequence" is often foreign to the child or irrelevant to the child's interest. Where, for example, the adult makes a point of turning off the TV set and then turning on the stereo, the child may, and often does, ignore the sequence. The child who is learning how to dress himself is a prime example of an individual who does not know what the proper sequence is— putting his shoes on and then noticing his socks on the side of the bed—or does not care what the proper sequence is—the child who gets so involved in the fun of putting things on until there is nothing left in his closet.

Children engage in seemingly purposeless behavior. Children do not play because play will improve their motor skills or because play will teach them something about the values of competition and cooperation. They don't fool around because fooling around is a successful technique for dealing with tension and pressure. The reason that children play is only that they want to; it is fun. Playing, fooling around, making faces, or standing on one's head do or may come equipped with their own justifications, but a child runs because she feels like it. The adult runs in order to improve his cardiovascular fitness or because he is late for an appointment.

One of the prime examples of seemingly purposeless behavior that teachers come across all the time is daydreaming. Typically, teachers deal with daydreaming in one of four ways. First, they may punish it: "You will not daydream in my classroom." Second, they may try to disallow it: "Pay attention, please." Third, they may ignore it. Fourth, they may try to encourage it within very controlled circumstances. In effect, some teachers may incorporate daydreaming into the curriculum, saying to the children, "We give you these five (or ten or twenty) minutes a day to daydream. You are expected to do all of your daydreaming during that period. When you are in mathematics, therefore, we expect your full attention." We may agree or disagree with any or all of these methods. What we should realize, though, is that all of them, ranging from the most conservative to the most progressive, view the act of daydreaming in ways quite distinct from the way the child views that same act.

Children are rarely motivated by long-range goals. In general, if it is a goal for a child, if it *really* affects her behavior, then it is a short-range goal. Sit down sometime with a second-grader and explain to her that mathematics will be very important for her when she gets to high school, college, or what is euphemistically called the "real world." If you rely on this argument to convince the child to practice her addition, and if the child has no other reason for practicing her addition, the chances are enormously high that you will have a child on your hands who will not be able to count. Something else must be brought in, some reference to the child's short-term interest.

Children are almost always at a disadvantage in their dealings with adults. Moreover, they are at a disadvantage in a number of different, significant ways. As a class, they are less strong than adults. They must rely on the good grace of adults' established customs and laws, and on their own wiles. Intellectually, they are, generally, less capable than adults. The child is a novice to standard forms of argumentation and, subsequently, the chances that a child will be able to defend himself intellectually are as bad or worse than the chances that he will be physically capable of defending himself. Emotionally, children have not developed all the defenses, all the "armor," that characterize most adults. Although children can and do adopt a number of effective strategies for getting what they want and although we can accurately speak about a young child tyranizing a household, the brute fact remains that, to paraphrase James Thurber, in the war between children and adults, the casualty list for children will be disproportionately high.

Later, we will try to devise some rules for discourse, a set of ethical do's and don't's that can be applied to talking with children. At this point, however, it seems clear that adults, by virtue of their superior strength (physical, intellectual, and emotional), have certain obligations and restrictions placed on how they should talk and reason with children which are not placed on similar speech among adults. Thus, although *caveat interlocutor* might be an acceptable rule for adult discourse, it is not an acceptable rule for discourse among adults and children precisely because children are members of that class who cannot beware and who cannot take steps to protect themselves.

Children exist in a compulsory network. They are forced, by external authorities, to do that which they might not otherwise do. We accept this, and we chalk it up to the "nature of childhood." That is, children do not know what is good for children; therefore adults ought to make decisions for children.

At this point, there is no need to dispute this principle, although we might point out that if we accept it we should be prepared to say why a similar principle should not be applied to relations among adults—there are adults who do not know what is good for them. Rather, the only thing we need underscore here is that children exist in a network (a compulsory one) that is quite different from the one adults exist in. Adults, of course, can be forced by circumstances, by financial necessity, by prior conditioning, by conscious motivation, to do a whole host of things they would rather not do. Adults, however, rarely feel obligated to follow the day-to-day dictates of their parents. Children do have that sort of relationship with their parents, and the simple fact of this relationship is, it would seem, crucial to an attempt to improve the quality of talking that goes on between parents and children. Parents and children are not on an equal footing. If you want to have a free and productive exchange with your child, you must take some steps to ensure that, at least within the bounds of a given conversation, the child will be free from being compelled by the parents and that the parents will be free from compelling the child, in any direction or toward any conclusion.

Now, I am not arguing for a complete overhaul of parent-child relationships. Quite often parents do know what is best for children, and it would be a mistake to allow the child to do only as she pleases. I am arguing, quite simply, that to *force* a child to reason in a certain way, or believe a certain way, or talk a certain way will preclude both parent and child from taking part in the sort of activities that are discussed throughout this book.

We want to talk with children in such a way that the speech somehow enables both adult and child to make more sense of their environment, to figure out how this is related to that and how that is related to those. There are obvious and not-so-obvious differences between adults and children that may aid or hinder that attempt. In this chapter, I have listed eight differences:

(1) Children are inexperienced. If experience is the "stuff" of reason, then children quite often do not have enough "stuff" to reason effectively. This is not the same as saying that children could not reason effectively even if they did have enough "stuff."

(2) Children are less effective users of language than adults. Children are in much the same boat as the traveler in a foreign country who does not speak the language of that land. Like that traveler, the child is handicapped in expressing himself.

(3) Children tend to think with their bodies. Adults locate consciousness "inside their heads." They can sit quietly and think about something. This does not seem to be an ability shared by many children.

(4) Children do not deal with their problems in the same way that adults usually do. Children have an ability (or disability) to disregard proper sequence.

(5) Children are often content to engage in activities that have no apparent end beyond the activities themselves. A child plays in order to play, not in order to improve her gross motor skills.

(6) Children are usually motivated by short-term goals. To tell a child that he should do this because this will help him when he is an adult is to give him little reason for performing the activity in question.

(7) Children are usually at a disadvantage in dealing with adults. Children are generally physically, intellectually, and emotionally weaker than adults.

(8) Children exist in "networks" that are quite distinct from the networks adults live in; they are told that they have an ethical and legal obligation to do what adults tell them to do.

I have not attempted to give an exhaustive list of the characteristics of children. Neither have I attempted to speak about what is "natural" to children. Rather, I simply tried to list characteristics that most children share. (One way to judge the accuracy of this list is to go out and talk with groups of children.) From this list, from this "look" at children, we will attempt to arrive at a set of guidelines that will facilitate talk between children and adults.

SOME RULES
OF
THE GAME

The movies are old now and rather dated. We watch them on late-night television and they, the early movies of James Dean and Marlon Brando, are heavy-handed. Brando is a caricature in *The Wild One.* Dean seems almost prissy in *Rebel Without a Cause.* Still there is something about those movies that draws us to them. There is something incredibly powerful about the performances of those two slightly post-adolescent actors in those two, what used to be called, "youth movies." Part of that power, it seems to me, relates to the way Dean and Brando used language.

When they were young, they had the ability to wrap themselves in cloaks of silence. When they did talk, when they mumbled something or other, the audience would lean forward, trying to catch what they said. The silence, I think, served two functions. On the other hand, it protected them from having to deal with all the inane dribble that gushed forth from the mouths of those around them. Dean and Brando could put on the "cloaks" and adult words could not touch them. On the other hand, when they did speak, Dean and Brando set the rules. If you wanted to talk to them, you had to play by their rules. You gave certain words a certain intonation. You used a specific shorthand. You paused here, but not there.

What is so interesting about Dean and Brando, especially for our purposes, is that they played the roles, in those movies, of frightened adolescents who had no defense but to swagger and bluff, and yet the characters they played were always on top of the conversational game and the other characters were always trying to keep up. Dean and Brando were in control.

If children had the same sort of conversational power, then we might simply say to children, *caveat interlocutor* and let it go at that. We would be justified in allowing the children to take care of themselves. But children do not have that sort of power and control. They do not use language and silence with the same sort of masterly skill that Dean and Brando did. Rather, they bluster into conversation and retreat into silences. For the most part, they, as we said in a previous chapter, are unskilled users of language. Because of this, it is incumbent on us as skilled language users to make sure, as much as possible, that the rights of children, linguistic and otherwise, are protected. We might, in a more enlightened time, set up a child protection agency whose task it would be to protect the rights of children and to shield them from foolish or unscrupulous talkers. Since we have not arrived at that stage of enlightenment, we will have to content ourselves with proposing a few rules that the intelligent and scrupulous adult might operate under when talking with children. These are meant to be general rules that are applicable to all talk between adults and children. In the following chapters, we will talk about specific kinds of talk and specific rules for those kinds of talk.

(1) Avoid being the "avenging angel." There should be an equivalent to the confessional seal—the seal that prevents a priest from using what he hears in the confessional against the penitent—on talk between parents and children. Of course, we want children to be honest, to tell the truth, and to accept the consequences of their actions. Still, if you want a child to "open up," she must have some reason to believe that it will not be completely disastrous for her to do so. The child has to have reason to believe that she can take a chance in the conversation, that there is some safety within the conversation, and that she will not be punished simply because she has said something that displeases her mother or father.

(2) Avoid browbeating the child. There can be a very important distinction between what a child says and what the same child believes. A child should have the freedom and the opportunity to put words together in somewhat novel ways. He should, within the bounds of a conversation, be allowed and, at times, be encouraged, to adopt different stances. For example, if you are talking with your son and he suddenly starts sounding like a character in some television situation comedy from your childhood, if he starts saying that girls are cute but weak, not very good at sports, and make good nurses but lousy doctors, your child might be better served if you refrained from hammering home the error of his belief. What the child says might not even be indicative of his belief. He may be, as it were, simply "trying on" certain conventions.

It is also a good idea to keep in mind that although talking is an activity that we perform and although it is and can be a very powerful tool, it is quite distinct from other kinds of activity. No action and no tangible product need flow from a given set of words. Indeed, if we are reasonable, a good deal of talk will precede activity. We think out loud, we think with our fellows, and *then* we act. Just as it would be a mistake to criticize a reporter's spelling or grammar while he is writing in his notebook, it may be a similar mistake to force the child to speak well or espouse the appropriate belief, whatever it may be. Sometimes it is better to give the reporter and the child sufficient leeway so that they can arrive at some defensible conclusion, which can in turn yield results—a good story, fair treatment of their peers.

(3) Avoid intimidating the child. It may not always seem that way—when you drive from school to piano lesson to baseball practice and it seems that you are simply the chauffeur to this very small but very busy child—but the real power in the relationship resides with the parent. The smart child, the crafty child can always manipulate, but what he manipulates is his parent's power.

Have you ever sat down with someone you knew was both brighter and verbally quicker than you? (If not, then either you are a genius or you have a very limited social life.) Remember how intimidated you were before the conversation, how hard it was even to make conversation? If you were lucky, the other person, through whatever means, put you at your ease. Her knowledge or quickness became a tool that you both could use within the course of the conversation. If, on the other hand, you were not lucky, her knowledge or quickness became a barricade to further talk. You became like the child in the classroom who is afraid to talk because he fears making a fool of himself.

When parents talk with children, this threat of intimidation is constant. The decent parent, of course, will not resort to intimidation or will resort to it only when other options are not available. (If, for example, your child is in real danger of doing severe harm to himself, intimidation might be worth a try.) Still, even when intimidation is not used, the threat of intimidation remains a constant. It is precisely this threat which you must minimize if you are serious about improving the talk that goes on between you and your child. I say "minimize" because to eradicate the threat would be to change the very nature of the parent-child relationship.

The obvious question, now, is how one goes about minimizing the threat. There is a whole grab bag of techniques that you might use. You could simply pay attention to the conversation. Imagine yourself as an observer and listen for threats, veiled or otherwise, that you make within the course of the conversation. You could ask the child if he felt intimidated during the conversation. You could have a friend listen to a conversation that you have with your child. He might see things that both you and your child miss. You could audiotape a conversation; better yet, you might videotape a conversation. Obviously, we can intimidate with a look as well as with a word. But these techniques may all appear a bit extreme. More practically, if you don't want a child to worry about a threat, give him good reason to believe that he will not be threatened.

(4) Avoid rhetoric. Around the time of Socrates, there was a group of people, the Sophists, who were skilled in argumentation. The Sophists went from household to household offering to teach the young how to become skilled in argumentation, how to make their cases, and how to get what they wanted. The Sophists were not particularly concerned with the rightness or wrongness of various positions. They said, in effect, that if there is a weak point in your argument (no matter what the argument is), we will show you how to patch it up or hide it. The Sophists turned rhetoric into, if not a science, then a high art.

There is nothing intrinsically wrong with rhetoric. As practiced by the Sophists, it was value-free. Moreover, the skilled use of rhetoric can be quite enjoyable. Forgetting about the rightness or wrongness of William F. Buckley's views on economics, it is enjoyable, it is fun to listen to him. As a tool, rhetoric can be put to some very good uses; we can use it to get ourselves out of some very dangerous situations. Yet whatever its value, masterful rhetoric is an unfair inclusion in conversations with children. The skilled rhetorician can get a child to agree to conclusions before the child has gone through all the reasoning steps herself. In effect, the glib talker substitutes his reasoning ability for the child's. The child's task is no longer to reason. It is to acquiesce.

We, some of us more than others, enjoy hearing ourselves talk. We applaud our own verbal forays. We like linguistic flourish. Remove rhetoric and you deprive ordinary conversation of a good deal of its richness. Yet when we talk with children this is one deprivation we should be prepared to live with. (Let us keep in mind that we are not talking about a total absence of rhetoric; as in previous rules, we only seek to minimize.) Children are not ready to lock horns with Buckley or John Kenneth Galbraith. We do them, and ourselves, a disservice by treating them as if they are ready for those sorts of battles.

(5) Avoid being a fountain of knowledge. Certainly, you know things and I know things. Certainly, when our children come to us with some questions, we should simply tell them the answers. There is, however, one big difficulty with answers: they often stop conversation and stop thinking. I get the answer to a question and no longer have to talk or think about it. Now, if your purpose is to encourage your child to talk and to think, you ought to consider carefully the types of answers you give your child and what effect those answers have on your child and on the conversations that you have with him.

Of course, I am not counseling you to withhold information from your child; I am saying that simply telling a child the answer might not be the best way of getting information across. If more than five percent of you can correctly identify Magellan, Vasco da Gama, and Ponce de Leon, it would be extremely surprising. We do not remember facts that were "drummed" into our heads, in part because they were simply given to us. We did not have to appropriate the information. We did not have to use the information. We only memorized the answer and gave it back to our teachers.

Alfred North Whitehead said that the most boring people are those who know many facts but are unable to relate those facts one to the others, who are unable to do things with what they know. To treat a child as an empty vessel waiting to be filled with facts may make you feel good, but there is little evidence to suppose that it does the child any good. In fact, a good deal of evidence supports the claim that it interferes with the development of talking and thinking skills. Talking and thinking are activities like bicycle riding or water skiing: you get good at them by doing them, by being an active participant.

A legitimate complaint, by the way, against many schools is that they give children almost no time to talk or to think. Schools, of course, play different roles in our society, and there is no reason they should operate under the same sorts of rules that I am suggesting for parents. Still, what goes on in school will have a significant effect on the kinds of conversation you can have with your child. Without being unduly alarmist, it seems clear that some schools can effectively sabotage all of your efforts to talk with children. Thus, it would seem that parents have an obligation to advocate that their children's schools have certain characteristics. We will deal with those characteristics in a later chapter.

(6) Avoid personal histories. This is a tricky one. One of the worst things about the death of our parents is that we can no longer talk with them. And one of the worst things about not being able to talk with them is that so much about them will remain closed to us. We look at a photograph of our parents taken decades ago. They are young and smiling. But what are they smiling about? What did they *want* that day in July? The photograph stands mute. It will not talk to us and we can't talk to it. Our curiosity is urgent. It seems the most natural of things to us. Indeed, when we meet people who are not curious about such things we tend to wonder about them.

Our children are curious about us as well, but it is clear they are not curious in the same way that we are curious about our deceased parents. Our children do not feel a sense of urgency about learning of our personal histories. A sense of the past (and a feel for the future) is not something we are born with. It is simply a mistake to assume that children find what happened to you 20 years ago as interesting as you do. When your child asks specific questions, of course, you should answer him. As a rule, however, you should be wary of introducing personal anecdotes.

(7) Use analogies with care. One of the most important thinking skills that we can develop is the ability to think analogically—to figure out in what ways things are alike and can be treated in similar fashion and in what ways things are different and should be treated in dissimilar ways. We can make a great deal of cognitive progress when we begin talking and thinking analogically. A crucial point to keep in mind, however, is that before we can make that sort of progress, we must do a good deal of groundwork. That is, before you can begin to draw analogies between, say, sports and businesses, you have to know a good deal about sports *and* about businesses.

Children, almost by definition, have not yet done the groundwork. To use analogies with children is to often divert their attention from the subject at hand. Rather than talking about sports and learning something about sports or talking about business and learning something about business, we draw the child into a comparison of two poorly defined concepts about which the child learns little, if anything. Moreover, he learns little about the effective use of analogical reasoning. (Analogical reasoning works well—we arrive at a "good" or a "strong" analogy—only when there are marked, important similarities between well-defined concepts.)

Now, I am not counseling you to avoid analogies entirely. The ability to reason analogically is important, and you should help your child to develop it, but there are some real problems and dangers with analogical reasoning. Beware of the dangers; beware of the traps that you and your child might fall into when you reason analogically.

(8) Avoid playing the role of the moralist. As parents, we have certain obligations to and aspirations for our children. We want them to learn the things that we think are important. We want them to have certain values, to believe in certain things, to act in certain ways, in short, to be this type of person and not that type. We are, of course, all different people, and what I want for my children may be quite different from what you want for yours. Still, it is difficult to imagine a parent who does not have certain goals for his children and who does not take active measures to ensure that his children turn out to be certain sorts of people. Prescriptions for determining which goals are appropriate—is it better to encourage your child to be, say, fair-minded or self interested?—and which methods are the most effective means of reaching those goals can best be left to others. What we are primarily concerned with here is how to facilitate talk between parents and children. One point that becomes apparent, with near sickening clarity, is that when the parent becomes a moralizer, talk stops.

The argument here is not against moralists. It is not against ethics or moral education. I am simply saying that when you play the role of the teacher or the moralist, chances are, you will stop the conversation. Note: some conversations should be stopped. We are not arguing in favor of interminable talk. Neither are we saying that the child should determine when and how talk should take place. Parents do on occasion have a right and an obligation to moralize. But the moralist, in some sense, is in possession of, the Right Answer. Moreover, the moralist is in possession of the appropriate means for arriving at that Answer. When the moralist talks to the child, the talk is subjugated to the Answer. If there were an easier way of getting the child to arrive at the Right Answer, say by inoculation, the moralist would take that way. The problem with moralizing is that the emphasis is not on the development of talking skills, and not coincidentally, talking skills are not developed.

(9) Talk about interesting things. Terms like "interest" and "relevance" were nearly murdered in the 1960s and early 1970s. Educators stressed the need to make things interesting for children. To, perhaps, oversimplify their position, they said "don't teach children multiplication or addition by drill and rote. Children are not interested in that kind of stuff." We should, according to those theorists, turn arithmetic into a game and give the children little rewards when they do well. As we all know, there has been a great reaction against this notion. Parents and educators have pointed out that some of the things children may not find interesting are vital for their success in later life. Arithmetic may be a pretty dull subject, but arithmetical skills are crucial in the daily conduct of our lives; whether you like it or not, you need them.

Now, it seems to me that there is something wrongheaded about this entire debate, that people have simply missed the boat. They have missed the boat because they are using an, at best, barbarous notion of interest. Educators, parents, and administrators often talk of "interest" as if it were a characteristic of things, as if it were a quality like "redness" or "hardness." They speak as if either a thing has the quality or the quality can be added to it—computers are interesting in and of themselves, but arithmetic has to be made interesting; it has to be "jazzed up."

This line of argument is barbarous, is wrongheaded because "interest" is a relational term. As John Dewey pointed out, the interest of a thing is really just a shorthand way of referring to the connection that exists between the person and the thing. Indeed, interest is that very connection. For me to say that I am more interested in baseball than gardening is to say that there is a stronger connection between me and baseball than there is between me and gardening. Stated in behavioral terms, if I am more interested in baseball than gardening, then given the choice (and everything else being equal), I would play baseball or talk about baseball rather than garden or talk about gardening. If your child is not interested in ballet or if you are not interested in ballet, I cannot think of any good reason for talking about it. This is not to say that ballet is unimportant or that you might not want to try to build a bridge from what you are interested in, say modern dance, to ballet, but until you are *both* interested in the subject at hand, little good is going to come from conversing about it.

I stress "both" in the previous sentence because it seems to me that talking is a relationship that we enter into, and that the talking relationship—especially the talking relationship between parent and child—is governed by the same sorts of rules as other relationships. One of those rules is, in effect, that each person be sincere. If you say you love me but are only toying with me, then we accuse you of some kind of bad faith. We criticize you for perverting the relationship, for "using" me. In a similar way, if you give your child the impression that you are really interested in talking about her relationships with her classmates when you are only interested in getting her to behave in a certain way (or if you are only trying to develop her thinking skills), then, I think, the child can legitimately accuse you of bad faith. You don't really "mean it." The counsel here is really to avoid tricks or deceit, no matter how well-intentioned, when you talk with your child. You need not, of course, be interested in the subject in the same way or to the same degree as your child. You may be interested in dance as a spectator while your child's interest may be more as partici-pant. Still, unless there is a real interest on *both* talkers' part, why talk about it?

One final note. I may have given the impression that if a child tends to talk about, say, swimming more than, say, bicy-cle riding then we have good reason to believe that the child is more interested in swimming than he is in bicycle riding. As a general rule, this is quite reliable, but there are obvious excep-tions. Sometimes, even in the warmest of environments, chil-dren may be afraid to mention something about, for example, sex or the death of a relative, while at the same time may desperately want to talk about it. Listening to what the child actually talks about will be of no help here. You will have to use other clues—changes in the child's behavior, changes in his or your environment, the child's age and other interests, etc. As always, rules and techniques can help, but being a parent, you are with your child and the specific situation in which you find yourselves is something that goes beyond rules and techniques. There is a craft to talking with your child. There is also an art. Books can help considerably with the former, but not all that much with the latter.

(10) Do not be afraid to talk about important things. Attitudes about sex and specifically the way we talk about sex with our children have changed rather dramatically. At one time, not too long ago, the child would sit down with the parent of the same sex, and the parent would talk vaguely about all the problems the child would encounter on the road to adulthood—the lecture usually took place at the onset of puberty although for many of us, especially women, it was a feature of the pre-wedding preparations (one picked out a gown and was told about sex). If the parent was too uncomfortable with the subject, the child would be handed a book, at least three decades old, and be told to "read this." More commonly, however, the child usually picked up all of his information and misinformation about sex from his cohorts.

The preferred method of sex education today seems to be one in which child and parent engage in an ongoing discussion of sexual matters. One talks about sex when the situation calls for it. It may be called for at age three as well as at age thirteen. The language and the complexity of the treatment will differ for the two ages, but children are ready and desirous of talking about sex a long time before the beginning of puberty.

A similar change, though one that is still in its infancy, is occurring in the way we talk with children about death. We assumed that death, particularly the death of a parent, was too overwhelming for a child to deal with effectively. We assumed that the child was best served by as little talk as possible. Thus, we gave the child a scenario—Mommy is not in pain anymore, it is all for the best, etc.—and thought that the scenario would somehow get the child through. Now, that scenario and similar ones are, to various degrees, helpful. They do give the child something to hold on to; they provide respite. They allow the child not to talk and not to think. But what she will need, at some point, is the opportunity to talk about the tragedy. Talk will not make death any less overwhelming. It will not, of course, change the event. But it is one of the ways, one of the most efficient ways, that people have of dealing with the tragic. We are beginning to realize the consequences of denying children the use of this tool.

It is not *just* questions about sex and death that children need to talk about and can profit from talking about. Children are precisely the sorts of people who have most need of and can most profit by approaching what philosophers consider the important questions. One need not be a philosopher, however, to notice that children, especially young children, are interested in talking about—although they will not use this terminology—the nature of good and evil, personal identity, freedom of the will, the nature and existence of God, the origin of the universe. It should not be surprising that children are interested in talking about these things *if* they can talk about them using their own language and not the jargon of philosophy or theology or science. Children are very much in the position of a traveler "deposited" in a strange country and told to make her way. The child is, almost literally, thrown into the world and is expected to make sense of her experience and to deal efficiently with her environment. She is expected to do this within the space of a few short years. (Much of the sense-making is expected to occur before she enters the formal school.) A prime way that the child accomplishes her tasks, a prime way that she begins to make sense and begins to deal with her environment is through talk with her parents and her peers. To say to the child, "this is too big or too important for you to talk about" is to leave her in a nonsensical position—you have asked her tacitly to make sense and then have put a blockade in front of her attempt.

I am not saying, of course, that children and parents can profitably talk about anything. It is hardly profitable to talk about nuclear physics when one knows nothing of physics. It does not make much sense to talk about multiplication when one knows nothing about addition. Certainly, some subjects are instrumental for other subjects, and before you can talk with profit about one you must talk about the other. But when the child must make sense of a larger issue, we as parents are obligated to talk with her about the instrumental subjects and to work our way up to the subjects we must approach.

(11) Pay attention to pace. Alfred North Whitehead said that the secret to education is pace. One needs to know when to go fast and when to go slow. Pace is also the secret to most of our endeavors. Certainly, it is the secret to running any race over 220 yards. It is the secret to the more technical aspects of love-making. Any comedian will tell you that pace or timing is the key to success. (Johnny Carson even builds comedy routines around the problems he has when his timing goes awry.)

A sense of pace is also crucial to effective talk between you and your child. But it is not something you can develop overnight; so don't expect your child to have developed one. Don't expect him to know when to speed things up and when to slow them down. For the most part, he will not have the expertise or the experience necessary to a sense of pace. The requirement for maintaining pace will rest squarely on your shoulders.

Two questions have probably sprung to mind. First, how do I know when there is a problem with the pace? Second, what do I do to rectify the problem? The answer to the first question is fairly easy. If you have started off with a topic that is interesting to you and your child, and if you are using language that is suitable to the talk (see rule 13), and if the talk breaks down, then there most likely is a problem with pace— you are either going too slow or too fast; you are not varying your speed, or as they say in comedy, your delivery. When you or your child lose the interest you began with, when you wish you were talking about anything but what you are talking about, then you have a severe problem with pace. You should do something before the problem becomes that severe.

But, the question of *what* to do is more difficult. I cannot provide a specific answer. You and your child are distinct individuals. That which may be too fast for me may be too slow for you and your child. Moreover, when you and your child talk, each exchange will be unique. Talking is a cumulative sort of thing. We don't want to repeat; we want to build. You are really the only one who can decide whether the pace is too fast or too slow. The more you talk and the more you pay attention to what counts as a successful conversation and what does not, the more you will develop a sense of timing. Experience is the great teacher here.

(12) Know when to stop. This rule naturally follows from the preceding one. In fact, a strong argument can be made in support of the claim that this is one of the most important ingredients in good timing; it is important enough to treat on its own.

Earlier, I said that I am not arguing in favor of interminable talk. Talk between you and your child will naturally drift from subject to subject and will permeate a number of different environments—you will talk about airplanes in the kitchen, on the way to the car, and in the car. Of course, what you want to do is to talk about airplanes only for as long as interest warrants it—talking with your child is not like teaching a class or giving a lecture. You cannot assume that you will be able to talk to the child in neat 50-minute portions. Talk is messy, and it is fitful. It does not fall into neat little patterns. If you talk about airplanes for more than a few minutes with a five-year-old, chances are you are talking too long. As children grow older, their ability to talk about a given subject over a period of time will increase, but it is the rare child, indeed it is the rare adult, who can talk about one subject for, say, an hour.

I am not counseling you to "watch the clock," to time your conversations and say, "It is 7:52, time to stop talking about airplanes and start talking about ice cream." But I am suggesting that you be aware of time when you talk with your child. The comedian's rule, "Always leave them wanting more," may be appropriate here. There is, after all, tomorrow. If you say it all today, tomorrow may turn out to be rather silent.

(13) Use language that is appropriate to the child. A few years ago, I was working with some children and trying to discover what sorts of thinking skills they had and what sorts of thinking skills could be developed at various ages. (The children I worked with ranged in age from five through nine.) To find out something about their thinking skills, I presented them with a game which asked them to state the relationship that obtains among possible things, probable things, and actual things. They seemed to me to be very bright, verbal children. In the course of the game, however, many of them said that all possible things are actual and that not all probable things are possible.

As I said, these were bright, verbal children. They knew that although it is possible that cartoon characters might exist outside the cartoons, they, in fact, do not. They also knew that if it was probable that their baseball team would win the championship then it was also possible that it could do so.

What I should have realized at the onset was that the children had no precise definitions of the terms ("probable," "possible," and "actual"), or if some did have relatively precise definitions, those definitions were not shared. When definitions are not shared, when we don't mean the same things by the words we use, we quite literally are speaking different languages. I was not justified in drawing any conclusions about the thinking skills of these children because differences in meanings or differences in definitions precluded me from talking with them. For me to say, for example, that the children were not capable of abstract reasoning on the basis of my conversation would be as arrogant and wrongheaded as saying that because Jean-Pierre cannot "complete" the syllogism "All men are mortal. Socrates is a man. Therefore . . .," Jean-Pierre is not skilled in deductive modes of reasoning. Poor Jean-Pierre may not speak English. Put the syllogism into his language and you can begin to draw some conclusions about the strength or weakness of his deductive powers.

To talk effectively with your child you must both be talking the same language. In effect, you have to build a community—a community where you and your child are somehow like-minded about the way various words will be used and what they will mean. The building of this community does not occur overnight. It is an ongoing process that takes a good deal of time. Indeed, it is a process that, if you are fortunate, will never end; it will last as long as the talkers are alive. New words and new uses for old words will constantly be introduced into your conversations. You will frequently have to stop and talk about the talk. "Here is a new word. What shall we mean by it and how shall we use it? Here is an old word but the conclusion you are drawing is quite novel. Are you sure that you *mean* what we have agreed to?" Questions like these should often arise.

(14) Do not talk down to your child. This is a very simple rule. Many adults tend to be condescending toward the very young and the very old. Conversations break down when one party begins to patronize the other. Children and the very old will not always realize that they are being patronized, but they will realize it often enough. The sheer possibility that they will do so is enough to justify our rule.

(15) Don't take straightforwardness, precision, and clarity to be essential to all talk between adults and children. Eavesdrop on two four-year-olds playing house on a rainy afternoon (rainy afternoons are the best times for eavesdropping on four-year-olds). The conversation sounds, at times, as if two distinct monologues about different subjects had been taped and spliced together. Those four-year-olds simply do not care about the same things that we do. They do not take straightforwardness, precision, and clarity to be virtues they should aim at in their discourse.

Now, it seems to me that these are virtues that the children *should* aim at and that we should encourage children in the practice of these virtues. And yet if children live in a linguistic world that "meanders," you are not going to get them out of it overnight. Just as you can effectively kill a child's interest in writing poetry by constantly correcting his grammar or kill his interest in dance by forcing him to get this step right before he proceeds to the next one, you can effectively kill a child's interest in talking and, specifically, in talking to *you* by forcing him to be always straightforward, precise, and clear. Attempt to practice those virtues yourself and *occasionally* encourage him to do the same, but don't make an issue of it. Take the meandering and the rest to be features of the terrain. You are going to have to live with it whether you like it or not. You might as well make the best of it.

(16) Do not be afraid of the light or the humorous touch. I am sure that I am not the only one who has noticed that it has taken me a good number of pages and sixteen rules—one more is coming—to advise you about linguistic behavior. (Do not bother to mention that someone has already prescribed a set of rules to govern all human behavior, and that there were only ten rules in that set. I have thought of that, too.) The amount of time I have taken to write this and the amount of time you have taken to read it indicate that we both take talking with our children to be a serious matter worthy of our time and effort.

But we must realize that well-considered rules, good intentions, reasoning, or talking itself do not guarantee truth. Simply, we can do our best and fail. And that, it seems to me, is one of the distinctive features of discourse. We would be well-served, therefore, to advance our claims, serious as they may be, with a light touch. There may be better ways to distinguish people from other animals, heads of lettuce, and rocks, but certainly pointing to the use and appreciation of humor is one of them. Hyenas, when they laugh, do not really see the humor of the situation. A dog may be man's best friend, but you can take him to a Woody Allen movie and he will never crack a smile. Rocks and heads of lettuce are notoriously glum. It is only people who can see the humor of a situation. Humor is a characteristically human attribute, and it is exclusive to the species. To be able to see the ridiculousness of a situation, to be able to see the humor in a situation, is an important step in avoiding being overwhelmed by a situation.

In your charge is a very unfinished person. (We are all, of course, unfinished. It is just that the child is generally more so.) A child is, in fact, a mass of potentialities coupled with a very few actualities. Your major task as a parent is to help your child become a full, healthy person—to become, in large part, what she can become. Whatever a full, healthy person may be, the ability to laugh and to smile and the ability to get others to laugh and to smile are important elements. As parents, then, we have an obligation to help our children develop senses of humor. (This sound very serious, I know; but there is nothing frivolous about the need.) Quite often, we can accomplish this task while talking with our child. We can share what we take to be humorous with her and she can share what she takes to be humorous with us. Besides, even in so serious a task as helping our children grow, there is something to be said for enjoying our conversations with them.

(17) Take steps to ensure that the child's other environments support the talking environment that you are attempting to create. We have been talking as if the talk you have with your child were a separate parcel of land, as if you were attempting to create a separate environment, an isolated talking environment. We can do this and we will continue to do this because it allows us to concentrate on talking. But, we have created an artificial instrument. Now, if this instrument is to continue to be useful, we should recognize that the talking environment is related to a whole host of other environments. Three of those environments are the home, the neighborhood, and the school. The talking environment you create with your child must coexist with these other locales; all of your child's environments exist on a continuum. They all have a significant effect on your child. Obviously, some environments, like cells gone mad, can become overly powerful. Literally, they can kill the other environments and severely damage your child. If the child's neighborhood and school environments constantly belittle him, or tell him that his opinion is worthless, or reinforce the idea that he has nothing important to say, then the chances of your creating a productive talking environment are slim. John Dewey said that if the larger community is counterproductive to the ideas of the school community, then the educator has a responsibility to seek to reform the larger community. Today, one of the biggest threats to the building of a parent-child talking environment comes from the school. If a child is not encouraged to talk in school, if he is given the impression that all of the answers are in the back of the book and that the reasoning and talking processes—*his* reasoning and *his* talking processes—are not important in reaching those answers, then chances are your attempts to create a talking environment will be in jeopardy. I suggest that if the school environment is counterproductive to the ideas of the parent-child talking environment, then the parent who is committed to building the latter sort of environment has a responsibility to reform the school environment. Dealing with this responsibility will occupy us in a later chapter.

These 17 rules are meant to help you in the building of a talking environment. The list is not meant to be exhaustive. Do not take the rules as a kind of straight-jacket. Rather, think of them as an old comfortable coat that you can put on or take off as the situation demands.

TWO
KINDS
OF TALK

On that television program where that unfortunate skier, week after week, tumbles down the mountain, the announcer speaks about "the infinite variety of sports, the thrill of victory, and the agony of defeat." There is also an infinite variety of talk. Much of it is agonizing, but some of it is thrilling. Sometimes we win when we talk; sometimes the talk is a total loss.

In this chapter, and in the one following, I will spend some time talking about various types of talk. The procedure I will use will be much the same as that used in the previous chapter. I will separate out various aspects of talking and speak about them as if they were separate events. This will enable us to focus on them more clearly. We should remember, however, that the world is hardly as tidy as we might like it to be. Sometimes these kinds of talk will overlap. Sometimes a talk may have many or all of the elements of more than one kind of talk. (Indeed, a rather strong case could be made to support the claim that all effective talk is composed of elements of many different types of talk.) The only thing we need commit ourselves to is the claim that, frequently, talks can best be characterized as more one type than another. Once we accept this claim, we can formulate what would count as success within a given type of talk. The painter or the mathematician knows when she is getting better in her endeavor because there are certain standards or criteria of successful performance. When she meets these standards, she is doing a good job. When she does not meet those standards, she is doing a poor job. Again, once we formulate the standards we will be able to say what counts as successful talk and what does not.

In this chapter, and the next, I will deal with five types of talk—talk for information, for discovery, for sharing feelings, for passing the time, and for specific action.

TALKING FOR INFORMATION

At first glance, one would assume that describing appropriate standards of success for this kind of talk would be a simple matter. Here is a paradigm case. It is late Saturday afternoon. You are sitting in the biggest, easiest chair you own trying to unwind from a busy week. Your daughter, who has been busy with her friends for most of the day, comes in and asks what time she has to be home for dinner. You tell her 5:45. She says, "See you then" and turns to leave. Before she can make it to the door, you ask, "Where will you be?" She says that she will be playing at Mandy's house and is out the door before you can respond.

If you are like most people, and if your family is like most families, then many of your conversations with your child will be like the one described above. You have some "packet" of information—what time dinner will be served, what the letters "R.B.I." stand for, what Grandma's maiden name is, how many stops on the subway between Sterling St. and Beverly Rd. The child wants that information. She asks you a question. When you respond, when you answer her question, she gets that information.

In the paradigm case presented above, we saw something that frequently occurs when we talk for information. Typically, though certainly not always, talk for information involves an exchange. I give you some information, and it is considered good manners for you then to reciprocate, in some sense to give me information in return. In our paradigm case, you gave your daughter information concerning the time for dinner. In exchange, she gave you information about her whereabouts before dinner. Even in less paradigmatic conversations exchanges occur. Quite often the person asking the original question must respond to a question before the original one can be answered. For example, if you ask me what "R.B.I." means it would be wise for me to question you, first, on what "run" means. If you do not know anything about baseball, the simple definition, "runs batted in," will not give you any meaningful information. The measure of success in talk for information, then, is straightforward enough. If the child gets the answer to her question, then the talk has been successful. If the conversation has turned into an exchange, if each talker has a question answered, the talk has been successful.

One thing we notice right away is that this kind of talk is brief, to the point, and oriented toward the getting of information. It is really not meant to disclose much about the personality or character of the talker. Harry uses Bill as an "information object," an object like a book or a television or a telephone. If there is an exchange, Bill does the same to Harry.

When we talk for information, we treat the other talker the same way that we treat the policeman who gives us information as to the shortest route to Larimer St., or the waitress who tells us what the soup of the day is. If the policeman begins to tell us about the problems he is having with his children or if the waitress gives us her opinion about John Updike's latest novel, we become impatient. We become impatient when we are not given immediately and directly the information we have asked for, when we are forced to detour from our goal.

Now that we know what counts as success—the transmission of information—we can list some characteristics of successful talk for information. First, the original question must be stated clearly enough that the questioner knows what is being asked and the person questioned knows both what is being asked and how best to answer. Yesterday, my daughter asked me, "How many years did it take me to become seven?" My immediate reply was "seven." She said that that was not what she meant. I thought for a while and then I said "One. You were six years old, and then it took you one year to become seven." She said that that was not what she meant either. I asked her what, exactly, she wanted to know. She said she was not sure, gave me a kiss, and went to her room. This conversation broke down because the questioner (my daughter) did not really know what she was asking. When we do not know what we are asking, no answer is likely to satisfy us. It also broke down because the person being questioned (me) did not know what was being asked, could not get the questioner to phrase the question in a more precise fashion, and, consequently could not figure out what would count as an adequate answer.

This is, of course, an extreme case. More often, the questioner has a good idea what she wants to know but phrases it in such a way that the person being questioned is, somehow, blocked from giving the answer. When I ask you "How much did George Washington weigh?" you cannot give me an answer because you do not know if my question is about George Washington the infant, George Washington the adolescent, or George Washington the president. I know that I am thinking about the 47-year-old man, but since I do not tell you this you cannot answer the question. When we talk for information, we have to be clear about our questions.

The second characteristic of successful talk for information is that the *answer* must be stated in such terms as the questioner can make sense of. Answers, of course, are always answers to specific questions, but they are also answers to specific *questioners*. And if I cannot make sense of your answer, then, strickly speaking, it is not an answer for me. You pull into your local service station with a car that is making noises reminiscent of the sound you hear when you shake a thermos bottle that has been dropped on the boardwalk. When in answer to your question, "How bad is it?" the mechanic replies that it is the drive shaft, he is answering your question only if you know what a drive shaft is, what it means for a drive shaft to "go," and that when a drive shaft goes, it is, indeed, very bad. Otherwise, he is not answering your question. He is taking you on a detour, and, if you are not persistent, you may not get an answer to your question until you receive the bill.

The third characteristic of successful talk for information is that the answers must be correct. How often do incorrect answers produce happy but misinformed questioners?

The fourth characteristic is that the conversation must be to the point. The economy called for in this kind of talk is typically absent, as we shall see, in the other kinds of talk. If I come to you with a specific question in mind, you should answer that question as briefly as possible. Then, if you want to talk about something else or if I want to talk about something else, we can get on with it. You do not want to be like the proverbial salesman who burdens the prospective buyer with an enormous amount of information before answering the basic question: "How much does it cost?" The salesman may be doing a great selling job, he may be overwhelming you with information, he may be breaking down your defenses, but he is doing all that by taking you through a gigantic detour—he is not talking for information. Rather, he is talking for a completely different purpose—he is talking in order to make a sale. In effect, you and he are having different types of conversation.

Before moving on to the fifth and final characteristic, it would be wise to reiterate that children are linguistically unsophisticated. If linguistically sophisticated adults can be manipulated so much that they will buy something they neither want nor need from a forceful salesperson, and if this can occur in the space of a detour from a talk for information, we can see that this detour can be extremely hazardous. We should think twice before putting the child through one.

The fifth characteristic of successful talk for information is that the questioner, besides receiving the asked-for information, also receives some clue as to the import of the information. Bits of information do not exist in isolation. They usually come, as it were, carrying some baggage. If we are standing in the laboratory, and you ask me what two chemicals one has to mix in order to get a third chemical, I would be doing you a disservice if I told you which chemicals were needed but did not tell you that the combination of those chemicals is highly volatile, and that you should be very careful when you handle it. In a similar manner, if I answer your question but do not let you know that the answer should be held in confidence, that it is a secret, I am, again, doing you (and likely myself) a disservice. In both cases, I am answering your question, but I am not giving you all the information you need to have. I may be fulfilling the "letter" of the talk, but I certainly am not fulfilling the "spirit" of talk for information. Therefore, we ought to say that, in those two cases and in ones similar to them, the talk has not been successful.

We have spoken about successful talk for information. In simplified form, we have modeled success on something like this: question→correct answer. We know, as parents, that the world is hardly ever as simple as it appears in the pages of books. Quite often when our child asks us a question, we do not know the correct answer. What should we do then?

The first thing you should notice is that the talk has broken down. You do not know the answer. You are no longer engaged in a talk for information. Second, you should tell your child that you do not know the answer. I realize, of course, that this is not the easiest thing to do. It is not easy for us to admit our ignorance—especially to a child. The child views us as experts, and the temptation is always to act as experts even when we don't know the answer. This, of course, is a temptation we must resist.

Alfred North Whitehead said the job of the teacher is to get what he knows out in the open as quickly as possible so that he can exhibit himself in his real character: the character of an ignorant person. Once the teacher and the student arrive at that point, both can begin the interesting task of trying to learn something new. Whitehead's advice to teachers is appropriate for parents. Talk, in its fullest sense, is cumulative for both talkers. It adds something to the understanding of both. For me to get something out of the conversation, I must move beyond what I know; I must expand my knowledge. In a very real sense, talk for information becomes important precisely when it breaks down and forces us into other ways of talking.

Third, you should refer the child to the appropriate expert; that is, tell the child who or what to go to in order to get the answer. If the question is about microbiology and if you know nothing about microbiology, then have the child call your friend, David, who is a microbiologist. If the question is about the latitude of Aukland, and if you have forgotten everything you learned in fourth-grade geography class, then send your child to the nearest atlas. (Indeed, you both might go; knowing something about Aukland could come in handy.) The important thing is to help your child get the answer. If you cannot do it directly, by telling him the answer, you may be able to do it indirectly, by telling him where to find the answer.

The fourth thing you can do, if getting the answer immediately is not crucial, is to switch the kind of conversation you are having. You might begin to discuss wth your child how one would go about coming up with the correct answer or, indeed, what would count as a correct answer. Obviously, this is not something you would do if the question were pressing. However, in those cases, and there are many of them, where the question is not a pressing one, this is a technique that you can use with profit. You are starting with something that the child is already interested in. The only thing you have to do, and this certainly is a difficult thing, is build on that interest. At that point you will be doing what I call "talking for discovery."

TALKING FOR DISCOVERY

Let's go back, for just a moment, to some of the explicit and implicit assumptions of this book. We are assuming the following scenario: The world as it is presented to each individual does not make sense. We are assuming, with most developmental psychologists, that to speak of an infant's "world view" is to speak nonsense. The infant is confronted with a whirring, buzzing confusion. Her task is to make sense of this confusion; that is, both to discover the underlying order (to show that things are not as confused as they originally appeared) and to impose order where previously there was none (to show that things that are confused can be handled in an orderly fashion). In the first case, we may say that the child is in the process of trying to discover something. In the second case, the child is in the process of trying to invent something. When the child is engaged in either of these activities we may say that she is trying to make sense of her world.

One of the prime ways that children go about figuring things out is by talking. At this point, figuring things out takes on a social aspect. The child is no longer a solitary individual facing, as it were, the universe. She can begin to use other people's perceptions, other people's *meanings,* as a way of building her own. At first, the child may simply appropriate those meanings: "Daddy says that this is bad; therefore, I say that this is bad." Later on, she will begin to use other people's assertions in a more critical fashion: "Daddy, you say that cigarette smoking is bad. But pipe smoking is just like cigarette smoking, and you say that pipe smoking is not bad." At any rate, when the child talks to you, she receives a whole set of ways of dealing with her experience. In effect, she can use your experiences (and your mistakes) as instruments for dealing with her own experiences. Moreover, insofar as you are representative of your culture, the child can use the entire experience of the culture as a way of dealing with her own experiences. Talk with you can give your child entrance into the larger community. It can give your child the opportunity to share in the beliefs, values, and aspirations of the larger community.

It was easy to give a nice, clear paradigm of talk for information. Indeed, it took only a few short lines to do so. It is not, however, as easy to do the same for talk for discovery and invention. That is because talk for discovery is far less tidy, but far more interesting, than talk for information. Making sense of our experience is never an easy task. It should come as no surprise, then, that talk which aids in that endeavor may and will become quite complex.

As we discussed earlier, we cannot assume that children cannot handle complex matters. We simply do not know enough about children to warrant such an assertion. Nor can we assume that if the subject matter is complex the language used to deal with it must be complex. F. Scott Fitzgerald dealt with some extremely complex issues, and yet his writing is a mixture of elegance and simplicity. We would be well-served if we all strove for that Fitzgerald-like elegance and simplicity in our discussions of all matters. It would also be best were we to follow what we might call the "performance rule." If you are not sure whether your child is capable of talking about something, the best way to find out is to engage him in a conversation about it. If he cannot talk effectively about it and if you still feel the subject is worth talking about, you might want to try different approaches. In this way you may find a thread leading from what he already knows. Now, on to the paradigm.

You are strolling through the shopping center with your daughter, Rebecca. She is seven years old and enjoys strolling through shopping centers because she likes to browse in book, record, and pet stores. For months, there have been signs announcing the opening of a new pet store, and every time you have been at the shopping center, some construction in the store was underway. Today is opening day. Patti Page's "How Much Is That Doggie In the Window" blares from loudspeakers set up at the front of the store. Minstrels and jugglers block the corridor leading to other stores. You are drawn, pushed into the pet store.

Rebecca becomes enthralled, talking to a parrot. She is saying, variously, "What is your name?" and "Do you want a cracker?" The parrot—incredibly old and, if parrots can be weather-beaten, then weather-beaten—is saying over and over again, "Partner, bring the hay in." The inevitable question arrives on schedule. "Mommy, can we buy the parrot?" Lucky for you, you notice a sign that says that the parrot is not for sale. You answer, "No," point to the sign, and explain that the parrot is in the store only as a way of drawing people so that they will buy other things. Rebecca is disappointed, but she does have an answer to her question.

So far, you have had a nice, orderly talk for information. You have efficiently transferred a piece of information to Rebecca. We can say, therefore, that the original talk is now closed. What happens next is that Rebecca starts talking about the same subject, but now she talks about it in a different way. If you, mistakenly, think that she is still talking for information, you will block her path to discovery; you may stop her from figuring something out. But let us assume that you do not put that obstacle in her path. Let us imagine the following conversation:

REBECCA: Did you like the bird, Mommy?
MOTHER: Well, I thought she was interesting looking—
    interesting in the way some old movie stars are interesting

looking when you see them in the newspapers. When you see them without their movie star make-up, and they look almost, but not quite, like themselves.

REBECCA: But did you think she was pretty?

MOTHER: Yes. But pretty in a different sort of way. Not pretty like you. Pretty in an "older" sort of way, I guess. Does that make sense?

REBECCA: I think so. You mean sort of like the old peanut woman in the story.

MOTHER: What story?

REBECCA: You know the one—about Adam and Jeremy. Every day Jeremy sees this very old woman pushing a cart down the street. I think she was a peanut woman. She sold peanuts at the baseball stadium, and every day Jeremy would see her—every day there was a baseball game— and Jeremy would run from her. He was really afraid of her.

One day, after Jeremy had run home crying to his mother for the millionth time, his mother tried to find out why Jeremy was so afraid of her. I guess she wondered if the peanut woman was being mean to him. She'd never seen the peanut woman. She wasn't really sure that there *was* a real peanut woman. Jeremy had a big imagination; when you read the story, sometimes *you* wonder if the peanut woman is for real. Maybe Jeremy's just imagining her.

MOTHER: Is she real?

REBECCA: Yes.

MOTHER: Why was Jeremy so afraid of her?

REBECCA: Because of all the wrinkles on the peanut woman's face. There must be a million wrinkles on her face. She looks really mean. But it's not just the looking mean that scares Jeremy. It's the wrinkles. Jeremy is just a little kid, and he's never seen a face like that and it really scares him.

MOTHER: Is this a happy story? Does it have a happy ending? You know I hate sad endings. Does Jeremy make friends with the peanut woman?

REBECCA: Oh, yeah. It's really happy. One day, Adam and Jeremy were sitting on the porch—it wasn't their porch so they couldn't run inside the house—and the peanut woman got really close to them before they even knew it. When they looked up, she looked back at them. You should have seen the look on Jeremy's face. He looked like he saw a ghost. Then the peanut woman smiled at them. And when she did all of the lines in her face, the millions of lines in her face, went in a million different directions. The lines made her look nice and kind, like a good person. Jeremy looked at her and all of a sudden, he wasn't afraid. He liked her.

Then the peanut woman just waved, and Jeremy and Adam waved back, and then the peanut woman walked down the street. Nobody said anything. They were just happy. It's a nice story. I like it a lot.

MOTHER: Me, too.

REBECCA: Mommy, did you think that the parrot was smart?

MOTHER: Gee, I don't know. I hardly met the bird.

REBECCA: Mommy, don't try to be funny. You know what I mean. Do you think parrots are smart?

MOTHER: Well, it depends on what you're comparing them with. I don't think that they're as smart as most people. They may be as smart as some people—just a little joke. I don't think they're as smart as dogs. I don't think they're as smart as cats. I'll bet they're smarter than rhinoceroses or hippopotamuses. They certainly are not as smart as fish. Fish, you know, go to school—I'm sorry; I couldn't resist.

REBECCA: But why do you think all that stuff?

MOTHER: Well, let's try this. People are smarter than dogs and fish and parrots because people can do more things than dogs and fish and parrots. People can read books, magazines, and newspapers. They can read maps and figure out how far one place is from another and what is the best way of getting where they want to go. People can go to school—real school, not the kinds of school that fish go to—and learn how to read and write and do arithmetic.

REBECCA: But a lot of other animals can do a lot of things that people can't do. Fish can hold their breath for ever, and they never have to come up for air. They can stay underwater for as long as they want. Dogs can smell things and hear things that people can't hear. Elephants can remember everything that ever happened to them, and they live for a really long time. And birds can fly all by themselves, but people have to take airplanes.

MOTHER: That's right. I guess what I should have said is that people can do more of a certain sort of activity than other animals, so we say that they are smarter than animals.

REBECCA: What do you mean "a certain sort of activity?"

MOTHER: Well, I think it's something like this. We get . . .

REBECCA: Who is "we"?

MOTHER: People in general. Like when we talk about the people of the United States or the people of Mexico. People get together, and they decide that certain activities are important. Then we look around at various groups. If one group does more of the activities or if they are more developed than other groups, then we say that that group is smarter than the other.

REBECCA: But that's not fair. We just picked the stuff that we think is important, and it's also the stuff that we have, and then we say that we're the best . . .

MOTHER: But we're not talking about the best; we're talking about the smartest. There is a big difference there, isn't there?

REBECCA: Alright. But it still isn't fair. We pick the stuff that we think is important and that we just happen to be good at, and then we say that we are the smartest. But what if fish did the picking. They might say that being able to stay under water for a really long time is what makes you smart. Then fish would be the smart ones and people would be really dumb.

Or what if dogs did the picking? They might say that hearing things was really important. They might even say that running fast was important—then people would look *really* dumb.

MOTHER: You may be right. But that's all we have to go on. We really can't go to dogs and elephants and ask them what they think. They can't talk. We have to talk to "creatures" we can talk to. I'm not really sure what those activities are, but we decide that they're important, and if you do a lot of them, then we say that you're smart. And if you can't do a lot of them, then we say that you're not smart.

It's is not a bad idea to remember, too, that there is a difference between being smart and being the best. I am pretty sure that we can say which group of animals is smarter than the others. I am not all that sure we can say which groups of animals are better than the others. I'm not even sure that it makes sense to say that one group of animals is better than another.

REBECCA: Being able to do some things that other animals can't do is what makes us smarter than them?

MOTHER: Right. But you have to say which things. I know that birds can fly and people can't and that fish live underwater, and they don't get wrinkly, but . . .

REBECCA: But what *are* the things that people can do that are so great?

MOTHER: Well, like I said before, people can read, and write, and go to school . . .

REBECCA: Going to school is great?

MOTHER: And go to school and talk about going to school and try to find out what is so great about going to school. I think that's a really important difference. People can talk about things, and animals can't talk.

REBECCA: What about marlins?

MOTHER: What about marlins?

REBECCA: Sure, marlins can talk. We saw it on that zoo show. The one with the man you said was so old, but always looks the same. You said he's been doing that show since you were a little girl.

MOTHER: Oh, *Wild Kingdom*. Marlin Perkins. I'll bet he's older than the peanut woman. But he sure doesn't look it.

REBECCA: What about the marlins?

MOTHER: Dolphins; you mean dolphins.

REBECCA: No, they were marlins.

MOTHER: No, they were dolphins. But we can look it up later. But remember what Mr. Perkins said. He said that every day we're learning more and more about dolphins and that it *docs* seem that they have a language and that they do communicate—talk—with each other. I think he also said that we had underestimated the intelligence of dolphins. We thought they were just dumb fish—dumb mammals— and now that we're finding out they can talk, we should change our minds about them. The ability to talk is one of those important activities and when we find that a group of animals can talk, we should say that they're smarter than we thought they were.

REBECCA: I still think that they were marlins. But what about parrots?

MOTHER: What about parrots?

REBECCA: Are parrots smart?

MOTHER: No, I don't think so. At least not as smart as people or marlins. Dolphins. I mean dolphins.

REBECCA: But parrots can talk. And people have known that parrots can talk forever. Remember that book you told me about? The one you told me I should read when I get bigger? The one about the parrot?

MOTHER: It's not *about* a parrot. But it does have a parrot in it. *Treasure Island.*

REBECCA: Right, but what about parrots? Aren't parrots smart?

MOTHER: Well, I guess parrots can talk, but they don't talk the same way that people talk.

REBECCA: But that's cheating. First you said that talking was important. Now you say that people have to talk . . . that animals have to talk in a certain way if they are smart.

MOTHER: If we are to consider them to be smart. I didn't mean to be unfair, but I see your point. Like I said before, I'm not really sure about this. Maybe we should ask somebody else.

REBECCA: No, We can figure it out. Just tell me what you mean now.

The mother and daughter in this conversation are, of course, fictional. (It should be pointed out, however, that the dialogue is not all that contrived. Most of it is bits and pieces of various conversations that real parents have had with real children. What is contrived is that a number of those conversations have been strung together; this for the purpose of giving a fairly clear idea of what I mean by talking for discovery and invention.) This conversation is meant to do the same thing as the previous paradigm conversation in the section on talk for information. It is meant to give a clear example of what counts as talk for discovery. It is also meant to provide a model against which we can judge the talks for discovery that we have with our children.

Now, the first thing that we notice about this conversation is its length. We might say that economy in speech is always a virtue but still admit that it is far less important in this context than in talk for information. That Rebecca and her mother do not present their "cases" as compactly or briefly as possible is not held against them.

The second thing we notice is that the conversation meanders. If you look carefully at the conversation you will find that at least five separate topics are raised. Rebecca and her mother talk about a book Rebecca has read, they talk about aging and the way people look when they are aging, they talk about good reasons for maintaining given beliefs, they talk about being scared, and they talk about being smart.

The conversation, as real conversations tend to do, spills from one subject to the next. Sometimes one of the subtopics leads the speakers to talk about a different subtopic. Sometimes, the speakers reach a kind of closure on one subtopic and then move into another. Sometimes no closure is reached; the speakers simply move on. Finally, sometimes one of the speakers reminds the other (in this example, Rebecca usually reminds her mother) that there is some unfinished business, and both speakers return to a subtopic.

A point to keep in mind, and this is an extremely important one and one we tend to forget, is that the model of talk between parent and child is quite different from that between teacher and student. When you are talking to your child, you are not in a classroom. You don't have to cover a set amount of material within a set amount of time. The purpose of this kind of talk is to lead to similar talk. Discoveries are instruments for future discoveries. The importance of the discoveries in optics that led to the invention of the microscope is that the microscope has enabled us to make further discoveries in a world which, prior to the invention, was beyond our abilities to perceive.

This is not to say, of course, that when talking for discovery one should not stay on one topic. Do not be misled by the example into thinking that all conversations of this sort *must* spill from one topic to another. You and your child might be more comfortable with staying on topic. On the other hand, you might find the conversation between Rebecca and her mother a bit confining. You might think that too few topics were covered. Again, you and your child might be a good deal more flexible than Rebecca and her mother. When you are talking for discovery you must proceed in a way most comfortable for you and your child. However, you should keep in mind that you are trying to discover things. Chances are if you move too swiftly and try to cover too many topics you will not discover much. Moreover, like a child who is allowed to run wild in a candy store and suddenly finds that she can no longer bear the sight of candy, you and your child may find yourself becoming sick of talking.

Along with the meandering quality of the conversation is a notable lack of pressure to speak to the point. Rebecca does bring her mother back to the point at various times; the mother does the same for Rebecca. But between them, there seems to be an implicit understanding—a sort of civility, if you will—that people are quite different from machines. People, especially when they are engaged in ordinary conversation, must be allowed to say what they wish and in their own way. Just as when we enter into a marriage we must accept the character of the person we have married or the marriage will be in for some rough going, when we enter into a talking relationship we should be prepared to deal with the characteristic ways that the other person talks. This does not mean that we can't attempt to change the characters of either our marriage or talking partners. It means, simply, that if you want to have a successful marriage or talking relationship, you ought to realize that your partner has a right to be and act as himself or herself. Mount a frontal attack on the other person's characteristic ways of acting or talking and the chances that the marriage or talking relationship will remain healthy are slim.

Another thing that we notice about this conversation is that not all the leads are taken. There are a number of points where Rebecca's mother could have built on some comments that Rebecca made. Look back over the section on aging, wrinkles, and being afraid of somebody because of the way he looks. There are a large number of things that the mother could have done here. For example, what is the relationship between the way one person looks or dresses and the way another person reacts to him? Stated another way, do we ever have good reason to be afraid of somebody because of the way he looks or dresses? We want to say that Jeremy should not be afraid of the peanut woman just because of the way she looks, but what about these cases? Should we be afraid of the ski instructor who arrives at the ski lift on crutches? Should we be afraid of the men who are dressed as pirates and whose ship carries the Jolly Roger as we make a trip—use your imagination—in the eighteenth century from England to Spain? Should we be afraid of the barber whose hands shake and whose face is badly nicked from a poor attempt at shaving?

Questions of that sort could have given the conversation some interesting turns. One wishes that one could step into the conversation and say "Look, why don't you talk about this? Why don't you try to develop that? This would be interesting, and it would help you to make more sense of that." One can imagine Rebecca's mother hearing a tape recording of the conversation and wondering why they simply let a given subtopic drop. But the simple and often brutal fact is that there usually is a lot more that we could have or should have said. Indeed, we may comfort ourselves with the thought that a really good conversation always leaves a good deal unsaid. There is, as the homily tells us, always tomorrow.

We should take note of four other things about this conversation and, by extension, about all talks for discovery. The first is that a great deal of information is being exchanged. Rebecca and her mother are not doing what is justly and disparagingly called "armchair philosophy"; they are not simply spinning theories out of whole cloth. Rather, they are exchanging information. Indeed, one can diagram talks for discovery, and find that such talks are composed of a series of discrete talks for information. (They are not *just* composed of discrete talks for information, but of that and a good deal more.) Rebecca and her mother say what they know or believe to be true, and then, within the course of the conversation, attempt to go from what they know to something else. They attempt to *expand* what they know. The tricky part, and this is one of the things that makes talk for discovery so interesting, is that there is no logic for that expansion. That is, you can't simply follow a set of rules and be assured that you will always be expanding your knowledge. There is always the possibility, as Rebecca's mother is quite aware and frequently points out, that one may be adding mistakes—falsehoods, if you will—to what is known. The "expansion" may, in fact, muddy things. Still, the procedure used in this sort of talk involves an attempt to facilitate, as much as possible, an orderly progression from that which is known to that which is to be known. This sort of conversation is as far from a rap session, where talkers simply say whatever pops into their heads, as kissing one's sister, say, is from kissing one's lover. They are qualitatively distinct.

The second thing to note is that each partner really listens to the other. Rebecca really *hears* what her mother says and responds to her mother, and her mother does the same. One does not get the feeling that there is a hidden agenda or that the conversation is being manipulated for a certain purpose. The best way to get a "feel" for this sort of conversation is to compare it with "conversations" (the quotation marks are necessary here) which are, in fact, its polar opposite. Think of all those times that you sat in a classroom and tried to give the teacher the answer she was looking for. You uttered some words. If they were the right ones, then your teacher built on that answer. If they were the wrong ones, then, chances were, unless you had a really good teacher, she simply ignored your answer and kept questioning until you or somebody else supplied the right one. When Rebecca gives an answer, her mother responds to *that* answer. This makes the conversation a bit untidy. If you are serious about talking for discovery, you are going to have to learn to live with untidy conversations.

The third thing to note is that neither Rebecca nor her mother has what one might call a compulsion to correct. Both Rebecca and her mother make mistakes within the course of the conversation. They say things that, quite literally, are false. Sometimes, if either party thinks that the falsehood will hinder the progress of the conversation, an attempt to correct is made. But at other times, when the mistake is thought to be trivial or when the speakers feel that correcting the mistake will hinder the progress of the conversation both parties covertly agree to overlook the mistake. Rebecca says, for example, that elephants can remember everything that has happened to them. Her mother wisely overlooks this mistake because correcting it is not essential to the progress of the conversation. Rebecca has already made her case—that animals are capable of performing a number of activities that people cannot perform.

The fourth thing to note, and this is one of the most elusive qualities of all talk and all talkers, is that Rebecca's mother has what, in a previous section of this book, we called a light touch. She takes the subject (more properly, the subjects) quite seriously, but she does not take herself all that seriously. She is willing to admit that she does not know all the answers, that she may be making mistakes, and that, although she is doing her best, her best just may not be good enough. There is a playful quality to the tone of the mother's speech. The jokes that she attempts may be the sort that are typically called "groaners" but they indicate a warmth of character. Rebecca's tone matches her mother's. Indeed, her jokes are the same type as her mother's. There seems to be a like-mindedness between mother and child. They seem to agree implicitly about a number of things, which gives the conversation whatever humor or warmth it may contain. A good deal more than a simple cognitive exchange is going on here. Certainly, a cognitive exchange is taking place, but what makes mother and daughter want to continue with that exchange, and what makes us want to continue eavesdropping on that exchange, is something beyond the swapping of information. Borrowing a term from psychology, it is the *affective exchange* that is crucial to our continuing the cognitive exchange. If we are not enjoying the conversation, and if we have the chance of getting information from somebody else, we will likely put an end to the discussion. Trying to discover things is difficult. If it is also unenjoyable, then there is little reason to believe that your child (or you, for that matter) will want to do it.

That, for the most part, is what we can say about talk for discovery. Since our discussion, at times, resembled such a talk, it may be helpful to summarize our description. The following are characteristics of a talk whose main purpose is to propagate itself, to lead to more discovery.

(1) Talk for discovery is long and meandering.
(2) A number of distinct points are introduced and developed.
(3) Often, there may be no explicit connection among topics.
(4) "Leads" are frequently not taken.
(5) Not much pressure is applied to speak to the point.
(6) There is a marked absence of pontification. Both talkers are trying to learn something.
(7) Information is exchanged.
(8) Some conclusions are reached, though there is an open-ended quality to the discourse.
(9) Each partner listens to the other and attempts to respond in an appropriate manner.
(10) There is little compulsion to correct, or at least, that compulsion is frequently held in abeyance.
(11) There is a warmth and a lightness to the conversation. Each partner is aware that, and acts as if, the other partner is something more than a cognitive machine.

When talks for discovery go well, they will have, for the most part, these characteristics. When they do have these characteristics, the talkers will discover things and will be encouraged to talk more in a similar vein. When talks for discovery do not go well, when they are unsuccessful, they will be missing many or all of these characteristics. In this case, either or both of the partners may feel that they are trapped in a ghastly charade and, if they have the power, they will stop it. The sad part about being a child is that one frequently does not have that power. Consequently, if you as a parent are serious about talking for discovery, you ought to do everything in your power to ensure that no charades take place. The guidelines in this chapter are meant to help you in that endeavor. Talk for discovery can be a very powerful tool, but as with all powerful tools, you ought to be careful in handling it.

MORE
TALK

If you look closely, you will see that this book is modeled, for the most part, on talk for discovery. In a sense, I am trying to "listen" to you and respond to what you are thinking. You can probably guess that I take talk for discovery to be very interesting and important. Still, I realize that most of our time, even when we talk, is not spent in talking for discovery. To denigrate all of that other talk would be the height of foolishness. In their own ways, the following kinds of talk are just as important as talk for discovery and talk for information.

TALKING TO SHARE FEELINGS

Sometimes, we have little desire for a simple cognitive exchange. For the time, we have all the answers we need. We do not want to talk for information. Neither do we want to discover or invent things. Certainly, making sense of this world is a full-time job, but even the sternest of employers give their employees a holiday. Sometimes, we simply want to express our feelings about something or to hear how someone else feels about something.

It is very hard for us as parents to engage in this kind of talk successfully, to allow our children to express some feeling or, in turn, to share some feelings with them. We do not want our children to hurt. Thus, when they start expressing some pain, we immediately try to soothe or protect them. We try to fix it, to make it better. The difficulty here is twofold. First, expressing the pain may be a necessary condition for coming to terms with it. If I can't express the pain I feel at the death of a loved one, then I probably won't be able to deal adequately with the pain. Second, if we do not allow our children to express their emotions we may misinterpret the signals they give us. We may think our son is experiencing a feeling of loss when, in fact, he is experiencing a good deal of rage. Our well-meaning efforts may only intensify that rage.

Another reason we often find it so difficult to allow children to express their emotions is that we think certain feelings are somehow inappropriate to children. I am not, of course, just talking about sexual matters although I will grant that listening to your child talk about how he really feels about sex can be a disquieting matter—especially if your son looks like something out of Norman Rockwell but reveals, or attempts to reveal, that Professor Freud had a more accurate picture than Mr. Rockwell. The problem of allowing our children to express their real feelings, rather than only those we expect them to have, is more general and relates to the image we have of the child and what sort of person we want him to be. When the child gives us any indication that he is not exactly what we want him to be, when, for example, he begins to show that he does not feel kindly disposed toward his sister or, say, to a family of a race different from his own, our tendency, as parents, is to correct him immediately. We let him know in no uncertain terms that this is the wrong way to feel. It is quite understandable that, as parents, we would do this; however, we should realize that this may not be the most effective way, if it is effective at all, of getting your child to change the way he feels about something. Most importantly for our purposes, this technique does not allow the child to express some feeling which he does in fact have. It effectively terminates his attempt to share.

Finally, it may be very hard for us to express our real feelings to our children. Just as we have an ideal image of our children, we have an ideal image of ourselves. We may feel that it is our responsibility to support our child emotionally, and yet there may be times when we do not feel supportive, when we don't feel capable of offering support. Now, certainly, we ought not burden our children with all of our feelings. It would be a mistake to treat your child as if she were a rather short therapist. Still, at times there may be very good reasons for expressing your feelings to your child, though the expression of those feelings might shake the image you think your child should have of you. For example, if you are anything like the rest of the world, you will frequently be afraid of things; occasionally you will be, quite literally, terrified of things. For you consistently to hide those feelings from your child is to present her with a picture of parenthood, of adulthood, which is grossly misleading. Moreover, it is a picture that your child, if *she* is anything like the rest of the world, will not be able to live up to. You need not bare your soul at every moment; obviously, a great deal of prudence is appropriate. But, while a little honesty may shake your image, the price seems worth it.

The following is a paradigm case of talk for sharing. Like the previous paradigms, it is not meant to be and does not purport to be a transcript of an actual conversation; rather, it is meant to be "typical." It is composed of bits and pieces of actual conversations.

Adam and his father are driving home from a baseball game. Adam is ten years old, likes to play baseball, and is good at it. Tonight, however, has been a terrible night for him. His coach moved him to left field and put his son in Adam's preferred position, second base. He also inserted his son at the beginning of the batting order and moved Adam down to the eighth spot. To make matters worse, Adam's play this night reflected his depression. He made an error in left field; he was sulking and did not see the ball hit his way until it bounced past him. Then, when he was brought in to replace the coach's son, who was put in to pitch when the starting pitcher complained of a stomach ache, Adam made a couple of throwing errors and failed to back up the shortstop on a throw from the catcher. Defensively, Adam was directly responsible for giving up four runs. Offensively, he did not fare much better. He struck out twice, but got on base one time when he was hit by a pitched ball. Unfortunately, he attempted to steal second base and was thrown out by the catcher. It has been a miserable night for Adam. Adam's father feels almost as bad as his son. He has had similar days, both as a child and as an adult, in baseball and outside of baseball. He knows how his son feels and commiserates.

It is about five miles from the field to their home. Adam's father attempts a trick that always works for Henry Fonda in those candy commercials. He substitutes ice cream for candy and offers to buy his son a cone. Adam accepts, but his mood does not brighten much.

FATHER: It could have been worse.

ADAM: There's no way it could have been worse. I stunk.

FATHER: Well they could have hit more balls your way; you could have come up to bat more.

ADAM: That's not funny. It was embarrassing out there. I felt like the worst player in the world. I wanted to die. I hate this team. I hate the coach. It's all the coach's fault.

FATHER: All the coach's fault?

ADAM: Sure, if he didn't move me to left field, none of this would have happened. Everybody knows that you put the worst fielders in the outfield and you put the worst outfielders in left field. Everybody was laughing at me when I went out to play left field. Then he had me batting eighth. The only person I batted in front of was Mark Belanger, and he's the worst batter in the whole league. Last year, Mark didn't even swing at the ball. He was too afraid to swing. This year, he's a whole lot better—he swings at the ball, but he makes sure that the catcher already has it first. He wants to make sure he doesn't get hurt. That creep of a coach has me batting before Mark. I'll bet if Mark wasn't on our team, he would have made me bat ninth.

It's so unfair. I'm better than Bobby. He just let Bobby play because he's his son. Bobby's the one who really stinks. He's fat, and he can't run, and he doesn't even like to play baseball. He'd rather play soccer. But his father wants him to play baseball. So Bobby has to play.

FATHER: It really was a terrible night. I was coming back from the refreshment stand when that kid hit the ball to you in left field. You were lucky it didn't hit you in the head. You might think about wearing a helmet out there.

ADAM: Dad, it's not funny.

FATHER: I know. I was just trying to make you feel better. I thought a joke might help. Sometimes jokes don't work, huh?

ADAM: Yeah . . . I felt horrible. I really like baseball. I know I'm not a great baseball player. But I'm good and I *am* getting better. Then he put me out in left field. If you play left field you have to be terrible, everybody knows that.

FATHER: I know how you feel. But it's not really true that the worst players always play left field. Yogi Berra used to play left field. Stan Musial used to play left.

ADAM: Who?

FATHER: Look at your baseball cards. One of the best baseball players ever.

ADAM: But, Dad, that's in the big leagues. When kids play baseball they always put the worst player in left field. Look at any team, the worst player is always in left field.

FATHER: I don't know. Maybe this is the way it is now. It wasn't that way when I was a kid. And I can remember some really good players on teams that *you* have played who were out in left field. Besides, it could have been worse. You could have been on the bench.

ADAM: I probably would have dropped the bench.

FATHER: *(laughs)* You might have at that. *(Pause)* Is that what really has you upset? That everybody will think you're a lousy player?

ADAM: Yeah.

FATHER: Do you think the coach really thinks you are a lousy player?

ADAM: I guess so. He put me in left field.

FATHER: Then why do you think the coach was being unfair to you?

ADAM: What do you mean?

FATHER: Well, if the coach really thought you were a lousy

ballplayer then he wouldn't be unfair to you if he put you in left field. The fair thing, it seems to me, if he really thinks you are a lousy ballplayer is to put you out in left field. What do you think? Wouldn't that be the fair thing to do?

ADAM: I guess so. If I really thought that some kid was the worst player on the team, I'd put him in left field, too.

FATHER: So what really has you mad?

ADAM: That he treated me unfairly. I was so mad I wanted to hit him. I wanted to break a bat over his head. I wanted to cry.

FATHER: I know.

ADAM: He *knows* I'm better than Bobby. He watches us at practice. He sees us at practice. He sees that I'm a better fielder. Dad, I catch the ball. Bobby doesn't. He can throw better than me. See, I can admit that; I can be fair. Why can't he? But I can run faster, and I can hit better. You don't have to be a genius to see that. You just have to open your eyes and look, and the coach does all that. He knows what's going on. But he doesn't care. He wants to be unfair.

FATHER: I don't know about that.

ADAM: Do you really think that the coach doesn't really know that his son is a lousy player?

FATHER: Ad, I am really not sure.

ADAM: But what do you think?

FATHER: I think maybe we should talk to the coach.

ADAM: But I don't want to talk to the coach. I want to talk to you.

FATHER: O.K. Don't get hostile. I'll tell you what I think. Before I do, however, you should be aware of the fact that I may be a little prejudiced, right? I'm *your* father.

ADAM: O.K.

FATHER: I think your coach wants his son to become a good ballplayer. He knows that you become a good ballplayer by playing a position where there is a lot of action, where you get a good number of chances, where you get the practice you need in order to improve. So what he does is to put his son in a position that will give him that kind of experience. In this case, it is second base. So he puts his son at second base. He may not even have been thinking about you. I don't think he was. He was thinking about his son.

ADAM: Yeah. He was just thinking about his son. But what about me? He should have been thinking about me. That would have been fair. When you think about what is right for everybody and not just what is right for you or your son. Isn't that what fair is?

FATHER: Yeah, I think it is.

ADAM: Then the coach wasn't being fair, right?

FATHER: Well, if we have the situation right, if that is what he was really doing, then it looks like he wasn't being as fair as he could be.

ADAM: That's gotta be the way it is.

FATHER: It doesn't have to be that way. We're just guessing here. The coach *might* think his son is better than you.

ADAM: Dad!

FATHER: He might really think that. Of course, he'd be wrong, but being wrong is not the same as being unfair. I think we may owe it to the coach . . . I take that back. I think you may owe it to the coach to talk to him, to find out what really is going on.

ADAM: I don't want to talk to that guy.

FATHER: What else can you do? You don't want to quit the team do you?

ADAM: No, of course not. I want to play baseball. The season is half over. I'll never get on another team.

FATHER: But you still think you've been treated unfairly, right?

ADAM: I know it. I know I've been treated unfairly.

FATHER: You don't want it to continue, right?

ADAM: Of course not.

FATHER: Then why not talk to him? At least if you talk to him, you may be able to work things out. Keep sulking and you may really become a lousy ballplayer. Do you really want to go through another night like tonight?

ADAM: No. It was horrible.

There are marked similarities between talk for sharing and talk for discovery. This conversation between Adam and his father—and remember, we take this conversation to be typical of the genre—is a long, extended one. It meanders. The speakers weave from subtopic to subtopic, and one subtopic does not "follow" in any logical sense from another. The speakers are not obliged to talk about *this* because they have talked about *that*. In addition, not much of a premium is put on conciseness or speaking to the point. In no sort of conversation, with the possible exception of a conversation among comedians, is irrelevancy considered to be a virtue. Still, one realizes at times that going up "dead-ends" or following false leads goes with the territory.

The very purpose of talk for sharing is to express some feeling to someone else. Nothing follows from this. It does not follow, for example, that the speakers will figure something out or even that they will be better able to deal with the situation discussed. It doesn't even follow that the speakers will feel better as a result of the talk. Indeed, there may be times when expressing your feelings may make you feel so bad that, in terms of your mental health, you would be well-advised to refrain from talking. When a loved one dies, the pain may be so acute that talking could only make it worse. At that time, a judicious silence seems called for. However, if the speaker is ready to express her emotions then our original criterion of success applies. If the speaker succeeds in expressing her emotions, then the conversation is a success. The task of the listener, then, if he is concerned with making the conversation a successful one, is to aid the speaker in expressing her feelings. This means, in effect, that when you talk with your child and you are both concerned with talking for sharing, you have a special obligation to avoid manipulating the conversation to other ends. The temptation is always to use our conversations with our children as mechanisms for teaching some moral lesson. Moral lessons can be drawn from practically any situations. However, when your child is trying to express some feeling, chances are she will not be able to do so effectively if she finds that you feel the emotion is inappropriate or if her expression is cut short by a moral lesson.

On the other hand, you are not a psychotherapist. Simply asking over and over again, "What do you think about that?" or "How do you feel about that?" may be a good caricature of psychotherapeutic practice, but it is not talk for sharing. When we talk, *anytime* we talk with other people, an exchange takes place. I give you something—usually some bit of information—and, in turn, you give me something—usually another bit of information. Of course, one of the talkers may be dominant, but if there is no exchange, one of the speakers is, in fact, delivering a monologue. Again, this is not what I mean by "talk," much less talk for sharing.

In the conversation between Adam and his father, we see a number of significant exchanges. Adam's father is not an impartial observer. He is not and does not attempt to play the cool, uninvolved doctor. It is apparent from the conversation that the father feels very bad for his son, that he has been affected by his son's problems, and that he would like to help, but for the most part, there is not much he can do. The father does his best to help Adam express what he is feeling, but he does something more. He reacts to what he hears; he attempts to relate things one to the other in order to help Adam make sense of what has happened, and he offers his opinion on various matters. While supporting Adam, he *shares* information, opinions, beliefs with his son.

Before moving on, we should talk about one of the opinions Adam's father expresses. Adam asks his father if the coach is being unfair. The father makes a distinction between two types of motivation: being motivated by a desire to do that which is fair and being motivated by a desire to do that which best serves the interests of one's son. The distinction is an important one, and, given what we can gather from the conversation, we might say that Adam's father is correct. However, the distinction does not speak to Adam's question: was the coach being fair? The coach may, indeed, be motivated by a desire to do that which is best for his own son and still be guilty of grossly unfair actions. Fairness has something to do with how we treat everybody, not just the people we are closest to.

Adam, then, is quite right to continue questioning his father. But this is little comfort to his father. Adam puts his father in a very tricky position. If he answers his son truthfully (let us assume that Adam's father does think the coach is being unfair), the consequences might be quite dangerous. Moreover, the person most placed in danger might be Adam. Typically, adults have a good deal more flexibility than children; when adults find themselves in a position where they do not think much of an authority figure, they can find ways around that figure that children typically cannot. The adult who despises his boss can quit his job (I realize, of course, that other consid- erations might force him to remain on the job. Still, he has the freedom, vacuous though it may be, to quit). The child who despises his teacher cannot quit. Now, Adam is not compelled to play baseball, but he wants to play baseball and he is compelled to play for this coach (it is too late in the season to quit). If Adam thinks that his father thinks that the coach is unfair, chances are Adam's behavior will reflect that belief. Chances are that Adam will become disrespectful or disobe- dient to the coach, which will cause a number of problems for the coach and, in turn, for Adam. One thing the father does not want to do is to create more problems for his son, thus he is hesitant about answering the question.

These are very good reasons for being hesitant. However, as we listen to the dialogue we realize that Adam is not going to be satisfied with an evasion. His father will have to either tell the truth, lie, or bring the conversation to a close. Let's assume that one should neither lie nor terminate the conversation unless there are compelling reasons to do so—unless you have sufficient reason to believe that telling the truth might put your child in serious danger. For example, if a truck is speeding toward your child, it would be ridiculous to continue a conver- sation about being careful; you would simply push him out of the way. Niceties concerning truth or keeping conversations going are irrelevant at that point. Adam's father, obviously, has decided that the situation is not that critical. He decides to tell the truth, to say what he really believes, but he is quite deliberate and cautious in the way he expresses himself. He says, in effect, that he thinks the coach is being unfair but that Adam would also be unfair if he did not give the coach a chance to defend himself. He urges Adam to, at least, talk to the coach.

This may not solve the problem but one is hard-pressed to see what better solution they can arrive at.

One final comment is called for regarding the way the father expresses his feeling about the coach. The father gives the coach the benefit of the doubt, but he makes it clear that the coach could be wrong. He makes it clear that even an authority is fallible and can make mistakes. At the same time, he makes it clear that both he (the father) and Adam could be wrong, too. At first glance, this may be disquieting. We, as parents, want to instill in our children a proper respect for authorities. Our children don't always know what is best for them and should, therefore, respect those who do know what is best for them— parents, teachers, police officers, ministers, etc. But how can we best instill this respect? Is Adam's father supporting or undercutting the principle that children ought to respect authorities?

We really don't have enough information to answer that question conclusively. Indeed, we might have to wait to see how Adam acts toward the coach consequent to the conversation. We can say, however, that if you want to ensure that your child come eventually to distrust all authorities, then you ought to impress on him that authorities are always right. When he learns that authorities are in the same boat with the rest of us, when he learns that making mistakes is part of the human condition, he will probably begin to distrust all authorities. If you are really unlucky, he may begin by distrusting the authority closest at hand—you. Letting the child know that authorities can make mistakes might be the best thing you can do.

TALKING TO PASS THE TIME

There will be no example given of this kind of talk. This is the talk in which, as the term says, we spend much of our time. Like background music that is piped into elevators, talk for passing time permeates most of our waking lives. It is all around us, and we partake of it without realizing we are doing so. Moreover, it is quite fortunate for us that we can force it into the background; bringing it into the foreground would be deafening. In previous chapters, I spoke of the child's task: making sense of the "whirring, buzzing confusion" into which he is thrust. Put yourself into the middle of a crowd on a subway or in the lobby of a theater or at some sporting event. Listen, really listen, to all the words that are being uttered. Try to make sense of them. Even the purist composer who is most offended by it might find herself yearning for canned music. Musak is, at least, coherent.

When we compare talk for time-passing with other kinds of talk, it seems quite insignificant. If any sort of talk is pur-poseless, it would seem to be this one. Talk for time-passing would seem to be the question of etiquette in a world of the most urgent ethical dilemmas. But most of our lives revolve around, not the larger ethical issues, but the relatively trivial ones of etiquette and manners. Infrequently are we called to decide on the "big questions." (Indeed, their rarity is one of the things that makes them big.) Typically, we are called upon to decide the more mundane matters. We make decisions about the mundane every day.

Further, we try to turn matters of etiquette into habits. If we had always to be thinking about the mundane—should I use this fork or that one? should I go first or should I hold the door open for her?—we would be able to get very little else done. The adolescent, for example, who attends her first dinner party may have to concentrate so much on appropriate table manners that she can pay little attention to the food or the conversation. It would make very good sense for her to turn table manners into a habit that she can simply fall into so that she can concentrate on other matters.

Much of talk for time-passing can and does become habit-ual in this sense. We get in the car, drive our children to the movies or to a skating party, and we talk. The talk may be about the party, the weather, someone's favorite color, the ratio of people wearing cowboy hats to people driving pickup trucks, etc. We do not really pay attention to the conversation. If someone asks us, when we get out of the car, what we talked about, we probably will not be able to say. If someone asked us a week later what we had talked about during that car ride, we, justifiably, would look at him as if he were mad. Talk for time-passing is not meant to be remembered; it is meant to help us pass the time. Talk for time-passing is very much like turning on the car radio when you are driving to work. You don't pay much attention to the radio. You put it on, for the most part, because the sound that it makes is preferable to silence. But talk for time-passing is not something to be taken lightly. It is significant for many reasons.

(1) Talk for time-passing is an effective way of fighting boredom. You talk to your child while stuck in some traffic jam on a hot Thursday morning in July and the time passes quickly. Anything that can make the time spent in a traffic jam pass more easily is, it seems, worthy of commendation.

(2) Talk for time-passing is something that people simply do. It is conceivable, though not likely, that this kind of talking will go out of fashion, but until that occurs, for all but the odd misanthrope or hermit, to be civilized will be to engage in this kind of talk. I grant that it seems a bit over-blown to say that when you talk with your child simply to pass the time you are, somehow, inducting your child into twentieth-century civilization. It seems overblown, but it is not altogether inaccurate.

(3) Talk for time-passing is an effective way of exchanging information. Talk is the sort of activity that always has an object; we always talk *about* something. When you talk with your child, you constantly exchange bits of information. A good deal of that information is relatively trivial, but even the most trivial bits of information can be used at a later date.

(4) Talk for time-passing is one of the ways in which people create bonds. It is one of the ways that people get to know each other. I meet someone on an airplane. We begin talking about trivial matters—how to make the seat recline, which airline serves the best food. We exchange information about ourselves. At some point, I may find that I like this person, and if I am lucky, I may have made a friend. All of that inconsequential babbling that we and our children take part in on the drive from field to grocery to theater to home is like that.

In large part and in a very indirect way, we are building a relationship with that talk.

(5)   Talk for time-passing is, in itself, memorable. When we think of our parents we often remember the times we simply sat and talked with them—talking with your father sometime in the early morning hours while the rest of the family slept as you drove cross-country, talking with your mother as she made you a cup of instant coffee. We cannot remember what was said. Indeed, probably nothing of import was said. Still, we remember talking. These inconsequential talks are important and memorable for us, and other such talks will be memorable for our children. This alone is sufficient reason for talking to pass the time.

Allow me one more anecdote. One of the rituals around our house, when I was growing up, was this: On Friday evening, after the dishes were washed, my parents and I would sit and watch the *Lone Ranger*. My father and mother would sit on the couch. I would lie on my stomach in front of the twelve inch Dumont television. The *Lone Ranger* would come on. The William Tell Overture would blare from the little television. There would be a nice feeling, a warm feeling in the room. Sometimes, we would talk to the Ranger. We would give him advice or warn him of danger. Most of the time, however, our talk was limited to the commercials or came after the show. We passed some time with those words. For me, it was very significant.

(6)   Talk for time-passing provides the stuff of our other conversations. As we drive, as we have breakfast together, and as we walk to the park, we mention many of the topics that, at a later point, will provide the starting points of conversations. In a metaphorical sense, important topics may be said to germinate in our more mundane conversations. When they are ripe, we may begin to discover something about them. First, almost unconsciously, the topic becomes familiar to us. Then, when the time is ripe or when the need occurs, we focus our attention on the topic. At that point, our conversation will shift from talk for time-passing to one of the other types of talk.

(7)   Talk for time-passing is the principal way in which children develop oral language skills. We learn how to ride a

bicycle by being put back on the bicycle until we get it right. In a similar way, we learn how to talk by engaging in conversation until we can speak effectively. Since most of our talk is for time-passing, most of the oral language skills we develop are developed there. This, of course, is not done in a formal way; rather, the child learns, almost by osmosis, that certain ways of speaking will be effective and others will not. She learns, for example, that when she contradicts herself the conversation may and often does break down. Thus, since she often has a stake in the conversation, since she wants the conversation to continue, she will learn fairly quickly that she ought not contradict herself.

(8) Talk for time-passing can contain clues and cues. Now, one thing we don't want to do is to play at psychoanalysis with our children. We are not qualified for that task and, most importantly, as parents we have other roles to fill. Still, one doesn't have to be a follower of Freud to note that children have a tendency to drop the most significant of comments into the most mundane of conversations. None of us, neither children nor adults, is about to say, "Now we have had this type of conversation. It is about time that we move on to this other type of conversation." We simply do not do this. Various types of conversation just blend into each other. Frequently, we don't even realize there has been a shift until the shift has been made. Children, as all parents know, have a tendency to make that shift rather abruptly. They drop significant clues into talks for time-passing. You should be conscious that children do this and be prepared to deal with whatever clues are offered.

One final warning is appropriate. Most talk for time-passing *is* mundane. One way to kill this kind of talk is to make a habit of looking for significance, of reading hidden meaning into things. Talk for time-passing is important for all of the reasons listed above. It would be a shame if one went overboard on point (8). I am tempted to delete point (8) in order to decrease the chances that this type of talk, this very important type of talk, will be killed by an indiscriminate search for significance. Restraint is called for here. If you miss certain clues you will likely lose little; the clues will continue, and at some point you will pick up on them. Refusing to search *actively* for significance will, at least, keep talk for time-passing "healthy" and will enable you to talk again.

TALKING FOR A SPECIFIC ACTION

If talk for time-passing is the most common of talks between parent and child, talk for a specific action may be the most familiar. The child wants something. The parent does not want to give it to the child. The only thing that will make the child happy is to get what he wants. The parent refuses to budge.

This kind of talk is the one most likely to cause tears and hurt feelings. No one likes to get involved in this kind of talk, but if you are a parent there is no way to get around it. There is, however, a way to make it as painless as possible. In the following example seven-year-old Jeremy wants to ride his bicycle to school. Jeremy is just beginning the second grade.

JEREMY: I'm in second grade now, you know.

MOTHER: I noticed that.

JEREMY: It's fun to be in the second grade. I think I'm going to like it better. Better than the first grade.

MOTHER: Why?

JEREMY: 'Cause in second grade, you're not a little kid anymore. You get homework. The teachers treat you like you are big.

MOTHER: Good.

JEREMY: And the little kids look up to us. We're big kids now, and the little kids look up to us. Mrs. Saroyan says that we have to set an example for the little kids. We have to show them the right things to do. We can't fool around all the time because then they would think that that's the right thing to do.

MOTHER: And it's not.

JEREMY: No, it's not. *(Pause)* Mom, do you think that I'm a big kid?

MOTHER: Yes, I really do. And you're getting bigger every day.

JEREMY: Mom, can I ride my bike to school by myself?

MOTHER: No.

JEREMY: Mom!

MOTHER: Jeremy, we've had this conversation before.

JEREMY: Sure, I remember. But that was a long time ago. That was when I was little. Now I'm big. You just said I was big. Rebecca and Adam get to ride their bikes to school every day. They're big, and I'm big. Why can't I ride my bike to school?

MOTHER: Adam is in middle school, and your sister is in the fifth grade. They are a *lot* bigger than you. Also, Adam didn't get to ride his bike until he was in the fifth grade and Rebecca didn't get to ride hers until she was in the fourth grade.

JEREMY: That was just because they didn't want to.

MOTHER: They did too want to ride their bikes. Adam asked to ride his from the second day of kindergarten—I had, by the way, just this sort of conversation with him almost every day. Rebecca was just as bad.

JEREMY: Billy Spritzel, Neil Lucey, and Gene Attenborough ride their bikes. Everybody in second grade rides their bike to school.

MOTHER: Everybody?

JEREMY: Everybody.

MOTHER: What about Jane Fox?

JEREMY: Jane is a girl. But even a lot of girls ride their bikes to school. Ann Aspen rides her bike to school, and she's been doing it since the first grade.

MOTHER: Ann lives on the same block as the school. She doesn't have to cross any streets. She only has to ride about a hundred feet to get to school.

JEREMY: Mom, I want to ride my bike to school. You said that I was big. Why can't I ride my bike to school?

MOTHER: There are a number of reasons. Are you really interested in hearing them?

JEREMY: Of course, I am.

MOTHER: Well, the first reason, and this is really the most important, is that it is very dangerous. You would ride your bike for almost a mile. There are no sidewalks on

Holly Hollows. That means that you would have to ride in the street. And there is a lot of traffic on that street. In particular, there are a number of teenagers on that street. They jump into their cars and head off for school at the same time that you do. They are not as careful as they should be. If I had my way, I'd make them walk to school too.

JEREMY: But you can't boss them around. You can only boss me around.

MOTHER: That's not a very nice thing to say, and I don't like the way you said it.

JEREMY: I don't care.

MOTHER: Then, I don't care to continue talking.

JEREMY: I'm sorry.

MOTHER: O.K. If you are really interested in hearing my reasons then I'll tell you. But if you just want to argue, we might as well stop right now.

JEREMY: I'm interested in the reasons. Tell me the reasons, Mom.

MOTHER: Like I said, it is very dangerous on Holly Hollows. I know that I can't make the teenagers walk, but I do wish that they would be more careful. Don't you?

JEREMY: I guess. But everybody else's mother lets them ride to school. Gene Attenborough's mother lets him ride to school.

MOTHER: Gene lives two blocks from school, Jeremy.

JEREMY: But his mother let him ride to school last year and Gene can't ride his bike near as good as me. He falls off every time he hits a bump, and he doesn't know how to fix his bike. He gets flat tires, and he can't fix them. His mother has to take the bike to the bicycle store, and the man fixes it. He must get a flat every week. That costs a lot of money. Taking it to the store every week. His mother must get really mad. Gene should know how to fix his own tire if he's going to ride his bicycle to school every day.

MOTHER: Can you fix a flat tire?

JEREMY: You know I can't. But Adam fixes them good. Good as new. So it wouldn't cost us any money to get them fixed.

And if I rode my bicycle to school every day I'd be really careful so I wouldn't get a flat tire. But if I did, I'd take care of my tire myself. I wouldn't cost you any money. Adam could teach me. He said he would. And then I could fix them myself. So it wouldn't cost you any money. Can I ride my bicycle to school, then, Mom, please?

MOTHER: It is not the money that I'm worried about. It's the safety. I don't care that much about flat tires. What I really care about is you. There are a lot of dangerous streets between here and school. I don't want you to be run over by a car.

JEREMY: Mom, I *promise*. I won't get run over. I'll be really careful, and I'll obey all the safety rules.

MOTHER: That's not the kind of thing you can promise. *(Pause)* I'll try it one more time. School is a long way off and . . .

JEREMY: But, Mom . . .

MOTHER: Let me finish, alright? I let you talk. Now, you let me talk. O.K.?

JEREMY: O.K.

MOTHER: School is a long way off. You have to ride down some very dangerous streets.

JEREMY: They're not *that* dangerous.

MOTHER: *Jeremy,* I don't want to argue. You asked for some reasons. I'm giving them. You can either listen to them or you can go to your room. Understand?

JEREMY: I understand.

MOTHER: Alright. For the last time—and I mean it—school is very far from here. To get to school, you have to go over some very dangerous streets. You have to be a very good bike rider, and you have to be very careful and very responsible. I don't think that seven years old meets all of those requirements. I don't think that seven-year-olds are that good at riding bicycles, and I don't think that they are all that careful or responsible. I don't think that *you* are all that careful and responsible, and, although you are a pretty good rider now, I know that you will be a lot better when you are in the fourth grade. Until then, you are going to walk to school. I don't care what the other parents do.

You are my responsibility, and I have to do what I think is best for you. And I think that walking to school right now is the best thing for you. When you get older, we can talk about it some more.

JEREMY: Mom, *when* can I ride to school?

MOTHER: I don't know. Probably not before the fourth grade.

JEREMY: But that's not fair. I'll be the only one in the whole school who has to walk. Everybody will make fun of me.

MOTHER: That's it, Jeremy. The conversation is over. You have your answer, and that is the only answer you are going to get. I know you're not happy about it, but that's the best I can do. Now, I don't want to talk about it anymore. Is that clear?

JEREMY: Yes, but I still have one more question. Can I ask it, and then I won't ask any more questions?

MOTHER: Just one more question? Promise?

JEREMY: I promise.

MOTHER: Go ahead and ask.

JEREMY: You said that you don't really know when I'll be able to ride my bike to school. When are you going to know? What do I have to do to get to ride my bike to school? I could be an old man and you still might not let me ride to school.

MOTHER: You're getting carried away.

JEREMY: I'm not getting carried away. How would you like it if you had to wait for years and years to get to ride *your* bike to school? And then when you finally got to be real old and you went to ask *your* mother and every time you asked her she just said, "Not yet. You're not old enough."

MOTHER: Well, I wouldn't like that.

JEREMY: See?

MOTHER: But I'm not doing that to you.

JEREMY: Yes, you are. That's just what you are doing to me.

MOTHER: That is not what I'm doing, I'll tell you what I'm doing. And then we will stop this conversation. *(Pause)* When I think that you are old enough and responsible enough to ride to school, I will tell you. I don't want to be mean—and I know that you're thinking that's what I am now—I'm just doing what I think is best for you.

Since I am trying to give prototypes of each type of talk, I am precluded from giving a happy ending to this conversation. If we extended it a bit, we would see that Jeremy remains unconvinced and unhappy. Indeed, Jeremy will probably remain unhappy no matter what his mother says; no argument is likely to convince him. He will be satisfied with one and only one answer. If the mother is true to her word, the conversation will end in short order, and Jeremy, we may assume, will go off to his bedroom to sulk and bemoan his fate. If the mother allows the conversation to continue, she will soon find it has become hopelessly meaningless.

Now, the immediate questions arise. "What was so meaningful about that conversation?" "Did it not go round and round in circles with neither participant yielding or modifying his or her position?" Let me answer the second question first. Neither participant did give up his or her position. The mother does not want Jeremy to ride his bike to school while Jeremy wants to ride it to school. This is the position from which each started, and this is the position at which each ends. However, the conversation does not just turn "round and round." It meanders, but meandering, as we have seen, is characteristic of virtually all forms of conversation. In the course of the meandering, in the course of the conversation, the mother states her reasons, explains them, and amplifies them. Jeremy learns, if he is paying attention, why his mother does not want him to ride to school. His mother does not simply dictate her decision; neither does she simply state her reasons for that decision. She, as it were, imbeds those reasons into the conversational framework. She listens to her son and tries to make her answers fit his questions. She is not simply reciting the "party line," or if she is reciting the party line, she is trying to make it applicable to the specific questions Jeremy asks. This is not an easy task. One is always tempted in these sorts of situations to issue pronouncements or, in effect, to post the rules on the nearest door. One is especially tempted to do this when one realizes that the child may, in all probability, be listening for one and only one answer. This is a temptation that the mother overcomes. Her talk does not have the vigor or the clarity of a

pronouncement; it has an explanatory richness which it otherwise might not have.

Now we have to deal with the first and more difficult
question. If we assume that Jeremy was not really listening or
that he was only listening for the answer he wanted to hear,
and if we assume that Jeremy was not convinced by the argument his mother presented, why should the mother go through
all the bother of getting embroiled in this sort of conversation?
There seems to be very little payoff. In large part, it seems to be
a futile, meaningless exercise. One can well imagine the exasperated mother retreating to some safe haven in the house and
wondering why she ever let herself get involved in the conversation. In many cases, perhaps in most cases, we should not
involve ourselves in these conversations. When you have
explained your position in sufficient detail you ought to put an
end to this kind of talk. ("Sufficient detail," of course, is a tricky
concept. A simple rule of thumb would be that you have
explained your position in sufficient detail when your child
understands what you want her to understand. The individual
parent, aware of the situation and of her child, must be the
judge of when the child understands.) There really is very little
point in going on with a conversation beyond this point, or in
reworking old conversations. If interminable talk of other
sorts can be boring and counterproductive, interminable talk
of this sort can be lethal. It can, in fact, kill a relationship.

Let's assume that Jeremy's mother has not reached the
point of sufficient detail. The question still nags. Why involve
yourself in a conversation that both is painful and has little
chance of "connecting" with your listener or of getting him to
believe what you think he ought to believe? The first answer to
this question is that there always is the possibility, however
remote, that the child will listen to you, that he will understand
what you are saying, and that he will come to see the strength
of your arguments. I grant, of course, that in cases like the one
presented above, the chances of this are rather slim, but if you
stop and think for just a minute about the awesome responsibility parents have—the control one human being has over
another—it may appear to you, as it does to me, that a few
tears, a headache, and some hurt feelings might be worth the

effort. There are times when it may be in your child's best interest for you to bet on a longshot.

The second answer to this question is that talking is one of the prime ways we have of discovering what we believe and the reasons for that belief. Often, at least for many of us, we don't really know what we believe until we get involved in a conversation in which we are forced to deal with things that, for various reasons, we have always kept just below the surface of consciousness. For example, we talk about capital punishment. I have always thought that I am in favor of it. However, as we talk, I discover that I cannot really argue in favor of capital punishment. My heart, simply, is not in it. I discover, during the course of the conversation, that I am not in favor of capital punishment and that, in fact, I never have been. I have simply deluded myself into thinking that I was.

Or consider this example: I think that I am not in favor of capital punishment and I think I have a convincing argument in favor of its abolition. In the course of our discussion about that subject, I discover that my argument falls apart. I may not change my mind on capital punishment, but, if I am intellectually honest, I will have to come up with a new argument.

Similar things can happen when we talk for action with our children. We may discover that we do not believe something, or we may find out that the reasons for our beliefs are not all that strong. In the example of Jeremy and his mother, one gets the impression that Jeremy's mother is quite upset about the teenagers on Holly Hollows. If the situation is as bad as she says it is then she might rethink her position on allowing her other two children to ride to school. On the other hand, given a different wrinkle in the conversation she might discover that she is overreacting. In any case, the possibility remains that the parent may come to understand her position a bit better. Again, it is a longshot, but it may be in your best interest and, ultimately, in your child's to take the gamble.

The third reason to get involved in this sort of conversation is that you will be modeling a form of behavior that comes very close to being a paradigm form of rational behavior. In a very explicit way, you are showing your child what it means to be a rational person. A rational person is willing and able to give reasons for her actions. In effect, you are showing your child that you take the willingness and the ability to give reasons to be a good thing. This is not to say that one must give the same answers over and over again, but that showing that you value *reasoned* positions is a very effective way of getting your child to do the same.

The final answer we might give to the question is closely tied to the third. As parents, we are concerned with producing a child who is reasonable, honest, friendly, courageous, democratic, prudent, fair, etc.; we want our child to have a certain moral character. We may disagree on the specific character he should have. We may disagree on the virtue—is being fair more important than being charitable?—but even those who want their children only to be able to think for themselves and to make their own decisions want their children to "turn out" a certain way. This is the parental role. It may be disquieting to put it so bluntly, but if parents are not responsible, at least in part, for the moral education of their children then somebody else (peers, schools, churches, etc) will take over that responsibility.

We must ask how best to go about building moral character. Talk for action is successful when it leads to some kind of action. (Frequently, as we saw with Jeremy and his mother, the talk "leads" to action when the mother *announces* that it will: "We have talked. There will be no bicycle riding to school this year.") But even if this kind of talk leads to the right sort of action (we will not define what we mean by "right"), we cannot say that the child is acting morally. To act morally is to do the right thing for the right reason. We don't want our children to refrain from cheating, for example, just because the teacher is watching. We want them to refrain from cheating because there is something wrong with cheating. We want them to have certain attitudes toward cheating. We want them to value honesty.

While one can get children to act in certain ways relatively quickly and easily, it is not that easy to get children to have certain beliefs and attitudes. A parent can command an action; he can tell Johnny to go to his room and expect Johnny to do so. Parents can't, however, command a belief or an attitude; building beliefs and attitudes is not that sort of process. I can't command you to value democracy or the brotherhood of humanity. I can't force you to value the Constitution of the United States. At best, I can create an environment in which what I take to be the appropriate value, belief, or attitude has a chance to grow. Metaphorically, I can provide the soil, adequate light, and moisture, but I cannot command the seed to germinate.

Whenever you talk with your child, but particularly when you are talking for action, you create a talking environment. You are telling your child what you value and why you value it. You are, in fact, letting the child see what kind of moral character you have. It is this kind of contact, on a day-to-day basis, that will have an enormous effect on your child's moral character. This answer—that in the long run and in an admittedly amorphous way talk for action will have an effect on the child's moral character—provides, it seems to me, sufficient reason for engaging in talk for action.

In this and the previous chapter, I have tried to take this very unwieldy thing we call "talk" and divide it into manageable portions. We all classify things into little subcategories that we can deal with, but generally these are relatively artificial distinctions. We say that this is physics, and that is chemistry, and over there is biology. These distinctions, certainly, are important. They enable us to make progress, to understand, explain, and predict. What we should realize, however, is that the world is never as neat as a textbook presents it. The cells we see with our microscope hardly ever look like the diagrams in the text. (That is one reason many of us had so much trouble with freshman biology lab.) We became good in biology when we learned to relate the constructed diagrams to all the squiggly, squirming shapes that we could see. It is my hope that you will use my diagrams in talking with your squiggly, squirming children. It is also my hope that you will use my diagrams in order to build some diagrams of your own.

WHEN
TALK
BREAKS DOWN

We all know people who buy cars, never check the tire pressure, and never get flat tires. For those of us who faithfully check the tire pressure and still get flat tires, this seems extremely unjust. But this only points out that many rules are disguised probability statements. They say, in effect, that if you do this you will increase your chances of trouble-free driving. If you do not, you will decrease your chances. In a very real sense, those who take a cavalier attitude toward their tires and have no flats are lucky. They are beating the odds. When we are through envying and despising them, we will probably say that they are foolish. It is a mistake, we might say, to depend on luck or blind chance, when you can, without much difficulty, stack the odds in your favor. Those who tempt the Fates, in fact, are stupidly gambling with a major investment. What we would not say, however, is that they are doing something wrong. Stupid, certainly. Wrong, no. We do not hold them morally blameworthy. Here the analogy I will draw breaks down.

Children, for all the reasons we listed in the second chapter, are in a very dependent position. They depend, in general, on adults and, in particular, on parents. Their intellectual, emotional, and moral growth is a function of what their parents do. This is not to say, of course, that parents are the only ones responsible; obviously, there are a number of factors over which parents have little or no control. Still, parents play a pivotal role in the development of their children, and talking is one of the principal instruments parents can use in helping their children develop. When we trust to luck the care of our children's character, we are doing something that is more than merely stupid. We are doing something that is wrong.

The language that I have been using in this section is admittedly archaic. Indeed, outside of the occasional ethics textbook, it doesn't exist. I am simply trying to point out, in the most dramatic language possible, that when we talk to our children we are playing for extremely high stakes. How you feed your child is important. But how you talk to her may be just as important. If it is bad not to feed your child, it is also bad not to talk to her. Most of us talk with our children, and most of us do a fairly good job at it. But most of us are like that parent who inadvertently breaks some of the rules of nutrition. The child won't starve, but neither will she develop quite as strongly as she might have. In this chapter, I will try to point to some of the obstacles to good talk. In an earlier chapter, I have a list of general, first-order rules; the following will be of a more specific nature and will deal primarily with the inadvertent mistakes we make when we talk. Let's call the rules that cover these mistakes second-order ones. The second-order rules deal with the mechanics of effective talk. Like the first-order rules, second-order rules are different from, say, the rules you would find in a mathematics textbook. The rules of talk don't have the kind of vigor or exactness of the rules of mathematics. It is a mistake to demand more vigor than a subject can give, though we should demand as much as we can get. We can arrive at the second-order rules of talk by looking at informal logic books and grammar books and by listening to people talk, by observing what makes conversations work and what makes them fail.

It is quite easy to kill a conversation in non-linguistic ways. Remember the forbidding glare of your fourth grade teacher? Remember how that glare stilled your voice? You were so afraid, you could not speak. When we want to talk with our children, we must make sure that nothing that is the equivalent of that teacher's glare gets in the way of the conversation. This means that we have to create an environment in which the child is not afraid to speak and where he does not feel that he will be penalized for what he says or does not say.

Now, I would not argue that children should not be afraid of certain things or that they should not be punished for their wrongdoings. But if we want a child to talk about what is important to him, we must not put him in a position where he knows that he will be punished for what he says.

The environment that you will have to create is not characterized only by an absence of fear. The child should feel that you are interested in what she has to say and that you value her opinion. This does not mean, of course, that the child should expect you to agree with everything she says. As we saw in our paradigm conversations, parents and children often disagree. The child should feel that she is talking to another person and not just to an echo chamber. You can be interested in and value someone else's opinion while at the same time strongly disagreeing with it.

This environment, as we mentioned in an earlier chapter, is an ongoing creation, and it is largely non-linguistic. It comprises day-to-day actions, looks, responses, etc. It is not easy to create such an environment. (It is not easy to be a good parent.) But unless you *can* create this environment, the following second-order rules for talk will be of little help. If a child is afraid to talk, it won't make much difference if you are vague or ambiguous. The child simply will not be listening. Get the child over the fear; then you may find the following rules helpful.

There are things we do, usually inadvertently, that can bring a conversation to a sputtering halt. If we do these things when we talk for information, the information may not be passed along. If we do these things when we talk for discovery and invention, nothing may be discovered or invented. If we make these mistakes in the other types of conversations, we may not achieve our goals. They are all violations of what we have called second-order rules. Logicians have broken these mistakes, or fallacies, into various groups. Those groups have been given different labels—material fallacies, psychological fallacies, fallacies of presumption, fallacies of relevance, etc. It is not important that you know those labels or the ones I give you. The important point is that you be able to spot mistakes.

Read this chapter, remember what you will, and then listen carefully when you talk with your child. If something does not ring true, you might come back to this book to see what, if anything, is wrong with what you have heard. The list I offer will not be exhaustive, but it will deal with those mistakes that we typically make.

FORESTALLING DISAGREEMENT

Some things are "obvious"; some things "everyone knows"; some things "everyone can see." When we reason, we don't want to have to go back and cover old ground; we don't want repeatedly to reinvent the wheel. Thus, there is nothing wrong, in general, with using locutions like those mentioned above if, in fact, it is "obvious" that "everyone does know." It makes little sense, for example, to explain the law of gravity every time we tell our children to move their glasses of milk away from the edge of the table. Everyone *does* know what happens when a glass of milk, a table's edge, and a five-year-old come into contact. But some information taken as common knowledge is not "obvious." Everyone does not always know. Sometimes we make this mistake inadvertently; however, there are times when this tactic becomes a way of forcing someone to agree with us. If you tell me that something is obvious, I may agree with you just to avoid appearing ignorant.

There are three specific reasons to avoid this mistake when talking with your children. The first was alluded to above: when you forestall disagreement you load the cards against your child. Whether you know it or not, you are psychologically manipulating your child, coercing her into agreeing with you by means of a tactic she may not be aware of. If she were aware of it, she would legitimately resent it. We all resent being tricked into occupying a position we do not freely choose. Given the vulnerability of children, these tricks are doubly reprehensible.

The second reason relates to what we may call the ground of an argument. To start an argument, simply, with "Everyone knows that . . ." is a much weaker beginning than "You should vote for John for these reasons. . . ." The former simply assumes knowledge, while the latter tells you why it is legitimate to claim to know. You will never devise an argument that is assumption-free, but you can avoid the assumptions that forestall disagreement. Where you can avoid an assumption, you should avoid it in order to put the talk you have with your child on firmer ground.

The third reason relates to what educators call learning theory. Children tend to remember more and be better able to use those things they discover for themselves. The impact of your telling a child that it is obvious that cheating is wrong will remain minimal until she has discovered it for herself, until she has been wronged by a cheater.

MISLEADING ANALOGIES

Analogies are one of the most helpful reasoning devices. We take a case that we are familiar with, we say that this other case is just like the familiar one, and then we can use the same tactics on the new case that we used on the familiar one. The difficulty with this and all powerful tools is that they are quite dangerous when misused. Sometimes when we reason analogically, we fail to notice significant differences between the things compared. Now, whenever one reasons analogically, there will be differences; one does not compare identical things. One compares things that have certain similarities. In the 1960s, one's position on the war in Vietnam was dictated, in large part, by the analogies one accepted. If one said Vietnam was like World War II, one argued one way. If one said Vietnam was like Korea, one argued another way. And if one said Vietnam was like no other war waged by Americans, but was like wars waged by other countries, one argued another way. All of those analogies could not be apt. Some are weaker and more misleading than others. If, for example, the war in Vietnam was significantly like the Korean War, then it was significantly different from World War II. In that case, the analogy between Vietnam and World War II would be misleading; it would overlook significant differences.

Certainly, you ought not preclude your child from using analogies. Moreover, you should feel free to use analogies yourself. The important thing to keep in mind is that your child is just learning this way of dealing with problems. Here is an analogy you might find helpful: learning to use analogies is like learning to ride a bike. At the beginning, you have to go very slowly, pay attention to all the details, consciously try to avoid mistakes, etc. When you become good at riding a bicycle (or using analogies), you can go a bit faster, you don't have to pay attention to all of the details, and you can focus your attention on things other than potential mistakes.

When an analogy arises in a conversation you are having with your child, make sure that you *both* see the similarities and the dissimilarities between the things being compared. Do not be afraid of slowing the conversation down a bit. Getting the answer quickly, discovering or inventing something quickly, may be the sign of efficient conversation, but, as we have said before, speed is not a cardinal virtue. It is far better to sacrifice a little speed in order to gain more accuracy. Tortoises do win races.

ASSUMING THE CAUSE

This kind of mistake more frequently occurs when we are talking for discovery. In traditional logic texts this mistake goes under the name of "post hoc, ergo propter hoc," which means "after this, therefore because of this." We leap from a sequential relationship (this precedes that) to a causal relationship (this makes that happen). The most blatant example I can think of is the fool's perception of the rooster crowing just before dawn. If we are to believe the reports of farmers, the rooster's crowing and the rising of the sun occur in sequence; only a fool would maintain a causal connection between the two.

Of course, we don't often come across examples as blatant as this one. But we frequently do assume that a sequential connection is sufficient evidence to justify a claim that there is a causal connection. Now, quite often we have to do this. The medicine that was on the table a minute ago is now gone. Our two-year-old begins to choke. We move as quickly as we can from the sequential connection to the causal one. We may be wrong, but now is not the time to concern ourselves with questions of being right or wrong. If there is even the slightest chance that our child took the medicine, if there is only the most meager evidence, we want to be prepared.

But when we talk we are rarely under that kind of pressure. Nobody, we may assume, will choke to death if it takes us a few extra minutes to come up with an answer. We have the luxury of time. Even in talk for information, where brevity and conciseness are considered cardinal virtues, we would be well-advised to slow the conversation down a bit. We are, after all, talking for information, not misinformation.

ARGUING FROM THE BIG STICK

We have said repeatedly that children are in a very precarious position. They have little power. In effect, the only real power they have is to manipulate their parents' power. Because of this it is especially incumbent on parents to avoid the argument of the big stick.

I argue from the "big stick" when I force you to do something, or to say something, or to think something by threatening you with some harm if you do not do so. My threat becomes the sole reason for your compliance. The threat can be as obvious as "Drop one bomb on me and I will drop 12 bombs on you." It can be as subtle as "Say this and I will think less of you." The threat can be explicitly stated or conveyed to the listener in a more oblique fashion. The threat can be conveyed by words or by a tone, a glance, or a shrug. In any case, whenever I argue from the big stick, you get a message. And the message is always clear: cross me on this and you are in for trouble.

As parents, we at times, as we mentioned in an earlier chapter, find ourselves in the role of "avenging angel." The point to keep in mind, however, is that every time you play this role within the context of a conversation, you effectively end that conversation. Moreover, every time you threaten to take on that role, you effectively re-channel the conversation. Once the threat is made, the talking relationship between you and your child is dramatically altered. Where once you might have been active partners in an attempt at discovery, you now become adversaries or, at least, potential adversaries. Introduction of the threat changes the politics of the situation. The child is no longer a free and equal talker, but becomes a "subject" of the parent. In effect, you change in one moment a democratic talking environment into an authoritarian one. Again, this may be necessary at times, but it is something that should be avoided if at all possible.

At this point I can hear my critics brandishing terms like "liberal" and "permissive." Let me try to take the wind out of some sails. I am not saying that children should not be punished for their wrongdoings. Sure, they should. I am saying, however, that there are exceptions to almost all rules and that that rule (children should be punished for wrongdoings) has certain exceptions. When the child tells you that he has done something wrong, you ought to refrain from punishing him if the punishment will do more harm to the talking relationship than it will yield in benefits for the child. Just as there are times when you ought not correct a child's grammar, there are times when you ought not correct his behavior. In law we do not accept all evidence, but only that evidence gotten through certain, approved channels. Normally, we do not admit evidence gotten under duress, or confessions forced from suspects. I suggest that a similar rule be applied to, at least, talk for discovery and talk for sharing.

AVOIDING THE QUESTION

Children are very skilled in this art. Look at the following talk for time-passing between six-year-old Gene and his mother. They are driving to the zoo.

GENE: I can't wait till we get to the zoo. I love the elephants best. And the giraffes too. Giraffes are Daddy's favorite. Did you know that, Mommy?

MOTHER: I like the monkeys. The ones with the funny faces. Funny faces like yours.

GENE: I'm no monkey. You're a monkey. Want a banana?

MOTHER: No, I think I'll just continue drinking my coffee. *(Pause)* You and your brother sounded like monkeys last night. You were really having a time jumping from bed to bed, weren't you?

GENE: It was all Neil's fault. He couldn't go to the zoo, and he just wanted to get me in trouble. He always does that.

MOTHER: And you never try to get him in trouble?

GENE: Never. I'd never do that.

MOTHER: *(Laughs)* Anyway, did you get your bed put back together? Did you get the mattress on the frame? Is the room fixed up?

GENE: I worked on that room for the whole morning. I went over it from top to bottom. You wouldn't believe how hard I worked. I did. And Neil didn't do anything. He just sat there and laughed.

MOTHER: I don't want to talk about Neil; I just want to know about your room.

GENE: I told you. I worked on that room for the whole morning. You wouldn't. . . .

MOTHER: I know. I know. I wouldn't believe how hard you worked. I believe it. I believe it. Now, I just want to know whether the room is fixed up.

GENE: I did a really good job of fixing. How far is the zoo? Can we see the elephants first and then see the giraffes? We have to see the giraffes so we can tell Daddy that we saw the giraffes. Won't this be fun, Mommy?

MOTHER: It will be fun. We'll have a great time. But why do I get the feeling that you're avoiding the question?

GENE: I don't know, Mommy.

MOTHER: Is your room fixed?

GENE: You wouldn't even know it was messed up yesterday.

MOTHER: Is *everything* fixed?

GENE: Just about.

MOTHER: Just about? That means something is not fixed, right?

GENE: There was just one small thing. The leg to the bed is sort of bent. It's hard to make the bed now because every time I stand on it, it tips over.

The mother, in this situation, should be thankful that Gene does not have a waterbed. Gene has gone to a great deal of trouble to avoid answering certain questions. He has not explicitly deceived his mother. He is not lying to her, but there is some information that he prefers she not have. Thus, Gene tries to give the appearance of answering the question, he answers questions that are like but are not identical to the question asked, and then he tries to re-channel the conversation.

We have given a number of examples to support the claim that, when talking, people should be allowed to go off the topic. They should be allowed to introduce topics that are not relevant to the conversation. We do not, however, want to go overboard on this. If one of the talkers has a question that is important to him, then the other person has an obligation to deal with that question directly. In a previous section of this book, we introduced a concept called "good faith." You act in "good faith" when you play according to the rules *and* when that play is somehow intentional. If you are fair, your being fair must not be an accident. Gene is guilty of bad faith. He knows what his mother is after, but he does his best to avoid giving it to her. Gene, if he wants to act in good faith, should either give a direct answer to the question or come right out and say that he will not answer it. The mother, it seems to me, is right to push her question until she gets an answer. She has a legitimate question, and there is no compelling reason that she should allow Gene to sidestep it.

BEGGING THE QUESTION

We beg the question when we assume the truth of that which we are asked to prove. The following are examples of begging the question:

"How do you know that this burns?"
    "It is combustible."

"How do you know that this dissolves?"
    "It is soluble."

"How do you know that he is innocent?"
    "He is not guilty."

"How do you know people die?"
    "They are mortal."

When we beg the question, we do not advance the conversation at all. We simply substitute a synonym. We explain nothing.

This mistake appears in some of the more important talks for discovery that we have with our children. For example, assume that you and your daughter are trying to determine the right thing to do in a given situation. You beg the question if you conclude that the right thing to do is what all right-thinking people say you should do. This is like saying that hydrogen is combustible because it burns. It does not advance your assertion at all. What you and your daughter really want to know is what it is about an action that makes right-thinking people approve of it. Answer this question and you have increased your knowledge; allow yourself to be satisfied with the original answer and you have begged the question.

ARGUING FROM MORAL PURITY

Think of all the athletes, television and movie stars, politicians, and writers who have become spokespersons for various products. The makers of those products, one may assume, are banking on the notion that consumers who admire those people will make something like the following move: "Tom Ochs is a wonderful person. Wonderful people like and endorse wonderful things. Tom Ochs endorses Grue Shampoo. Grue Shampoo must be a wonderful thing."

When you stop and think about it, when you put the argument in that form, it is incredible to think that anyone would make that sort of move or that manufacturers would think people would be faddish enough to make that sort of move. But manufacturers do make this assumption about people. They do, after all, pay celebrities enormous amounts of money for their endorsements. Moreover, they seem to be right to do so; product sales do increase when one picks the appropriate salesperson.

One of the more important things you can do for your child, especially in terms of his future financial well-being, is to point out, in the course of your conversations, that there is a big difference between *what* is said and *who* has said it. It is a mistake to move from a statement about someone's character to a statement about the truth or falsity of what that person says. Wonderful people can endorse miserable products (though if they do it frequently and knowingly we might want to think again about how wonderful they are). Bad people can say good things. Smart people can say stupid things. Honest people can mislead. And so on.

JUMPING ON THE BANDWAGON

We have seen this argument in virtually all of the paradigm conversations. Children resort to this argument, it seems, more frequently than any other. The argument in structure has three steps: (1) Everyone does something; (2) I am just like everyone; therefore, (3) I should be allowed to do that thing. This is the primary argument Jeremy used when he tried to convince his mother to allow him to ride his bicycle to school.

This is a curious argument, and one wonders exactly how children view it. It is hard to believe that they all think the argument is persuasive. At times, one gets the feeling that many children know that this form of argumentation is not all that persuasive, but continue to use it because they feel that the simple accumulation of words will wear the parent down. (In this assumption, by the way, they are often right.) At any rate, jumping on the bandwagon or trying to impress one's listener by an appeal to large numbers, unless one is talking about the results of a popularity contest, is irrelevant to most arguments.

You should be prepared to point out to your child that: (1) the original statement may be false, i.e., everybody might *not* be doing that thing (typically, you find that to be the case); (2) even though everybody may be doing that thing, this does not show that it is the right thing to do; and (3) what is relevant to everybody else may not be relevant to your child—her case may have significant differences. The important thing to keep in mind with this mistake and with all the others, is that you must underscore the mistake for your child and show her *exactly* what is wrong with the pattern of argumentation.

MISUSING THE JOKE

By this point, you know how important I think humor is. Indeed, I would go so far as to say that if you refuse to use the light touch or if you refuse to see the funny side of things you will not be able to talk effectively with your child. I am not saying, of course, that you must have the temperament of Woody Allen to be a good parent. I only say that children see the joke in life; they see the banana peel we all step on and they laugh. It takes them a while to see that there is also something very tragic about that banana peel. Thus, if you want to "connect" with children, you ought to be able to see the joke, too. Don't worry if you don't laugh at all the same things your child does. Your child may be too young to understand your interest in *What's Up, Tiger Lily?* You may be too old to find the Smurfs engaging. However, if there is no meeting ground, if you never laugh at the same things—say, Dr. Seuss, Laurel and Hardy, or Abbott and Costello—then following all the rules I've given you will produce rather uninspired conversation. The use of humor in a conversation between parent and child is both an indicator that a worthwhile conversation is taking place and a mechanism for continuing and improving that conversation.

Having said all of this, we should also be aware that humor can be misused. Indeed, it is the prime reason that many conversations become derailed. You tell a joke, and it takes my mind off the topic at hand. We often do this when the conversation is about issues that have important emotional overtones.

We are talking about war or poverty or women's rights. Someone makes a joke, and the conversation subtly changes course. We were focused on one issue and our attention has been turned to another; we were very serious and intent, and now we are less so. The tone and texture of the conversation have been altered.

As I said before, sometimes the topics *should* be shifted and sometimes the tone and texture of the conversation should be altered. It does not follow, however, that all conversations should be changed in this way. There are times when we have to put the light touch aside. There are times when we should be serious and intent and when we should doggedly stay on our topic. At those times the use of humor is a mistake. We should forego the joke and live with the anxiety and tension.

What I have said so far has most direct application to talk among adults. It does, however, have some application to talk between parents and child. There are times, especially when we are talking for sharing feelings, when the light touch is not called for. There are times, simply, for somber conversations. To try to alleviate all of the child's suffering with a joke is often to force him to put on a brave mask when he is not feeling at all brave. This is forcing the child to engage in a game of deceit. It should be avoided.

OVERSIMPLIFICATION

Oversimplification is the curse of the schools. An incredible burden is placed on teachers. Teachers have a certain relationship to a curriculum; they must cover a certain amount of material in a limited amount of time. The grammar teacher must cover all the parts of speech by November 3rd. The history teacher must get up to the Crimean War by Christmas. The mathematics teacher must finish subtraction today because multiplication begins on Monday. There is a certain madness here. Part of the madness relates to the way children learn. Teaching is a relational sort of activity; a teacher can't cover the Crimean War unless the children are willing and able to cover it with him, unless they are ready to learn. To tell all the teachers in a school or a district or a state that they must cover the Crimean War by Christmas is to disregard all the significant differences among the students they are teaching.

The other, and for our purposes more important, part of the madness relates to the complexity of many issues. Virtually any issue can be simplified, put into ordinary language. Technical language can be translated into something more accessible; difficult or novel concepts can be explained in terms of familiar ones. There is nothing wrong with simplification. There is, however, something very wrong with oversimplification. When we oversimplify we distort. We do not just make the issue accessible, as we do when we simplify. On the contrary, we remove the issue altogether, replacing it with a bogus version. The high school teacher who must cover *The Great Gatsby* in two class periods can do nothing but oversimplify. She can mutter a few remarks about flaming youth and how the very rich are different from you and me. She cannot, however, really deal with the novel. She does not have the time. She can only misdirect her students' attention to an oversimplified version of Fitzgerald's work. If she is a good teacher, she will hope, with Mark Twain, that school will not get in the way of her students' education. She will hope that the students will not think the oversimplified version to be an accurate one.

Now, teachers have, as I have said, special constraints that present some justification, inadequate though it may be, for them to oversimplify things. However, when we talk with our children, we cannot fall back on that sort of justification. We are not bound by a curriculum. We do not have to cover a certain amount of ground in a certain amount of time. If we are serious about talking about a given subject, we can take as much time as the subject demands. A good story, a really good story—something like E. B. White's *Stuart Little*—will not be exhausted in one night's discussion. We will find ourselves coming back to that book and other good stories again and again. A good movie, something like Disney's *Bambi*, is rich in meaning and ripe for interpretation. Simply to smile at the cute little cartoon characters or to cry when man enters the forest and the animals flee in fright is to miss a great deal of the movie.

Before closing this section, one final point about complexity is in order. There is a feeling, often unstated, among many parents and educators, that children cannot handle complexity, that they need things tied into nice, neat bundles. As we have stated it, this feeling has two parts. The first says that children cannot handle complexity; the second is that they need things tied into nice, neat bundles. Let us deal with the second part first.

If your child is like mine, you have little reason to believe that she either needs or wants things to be tied into neat little bundles. Still, we can grant that most children do have a desire for a kind of order. Break their routine, allow them to miss a meal or two, or allow them to stay up well past their bedtimes and chances are you will have some cranky children on your hands. But we can say the same about most adults. The same thing happens to you and me when we miss a few meals or when we stay up too late, too often. We begin to crave order. Simply, most of us, adults and children, prefer order to disorder. Therefore, to make the general statement about children is to make a statement of little significance.

Similar things happen with the assertion that children cannot handle complexity. Certainly, some children can handle complex issues as well or better than most adults. For example, a child who can survive in Northern Ireland without becoming brutalized is, it seems to me, a child who has successfully dealt with an enormous amount of complexity. Still, children and adults typically have more problems with complex things than they have with simple ones. It does not follow, however, that neither children nor adults can handle complex matters. You become proficient in handling complex matters by dealing with them. One reason children may not be as good at dealing with complex matters as adults is that they have not had as much practice. This is no reason to shield them from all complexity; on the contrary, it seems a very good reason for introducing them to complexity. The world is a rather complex sort of place in which to live. If you can help your child to deal with that complexity in the course of your conversations then I would strongly advise you to do so.

The purpose of all of these rules—both the first-order and the second-order—is to help you when you talk with your child, to facilitate the conversation. All rules are instruments. They are the sorts of things that are meant to be used. Still, it would surprise me if there were not important exceptions to many of the rules I've given you. You and your child may be those exceptions. Feel free to change the rules as you go along. The only thing I suggest is this: ask yourself constantly whether you are making progress in your conversations, whether the new rules add anything of significance to the old rules. If they do, then follow them wholeheartedly.

TALKING
IN
GROUPS

Look back over all the conversations I have given you. You will notice something about them: they all involve two and only two speakers. I have used this type of conversation, first, because it was easier for me to make the points I was trying to make when I only had to deal with two people, and second, because the introduction of a third or fourth party would have increased the sheer bulk of the conversations. But many of our conversations with children involve more than two people. We often do not talk just with our son Adam. Frequently, older son Jeremy and daughter Rebecca are involved in the conversation. Also, when we talk with our children other adults may be involved, a spouse or a friend—sometimes a spouse can also be a friend.

In terms of simple theory, the addition of other speakers will have no effect on what we have said before. Practically speaking, however, the introduction of other speakers may increase the chances that the various talks will break down. In this section, we will talk about those practical dangers.

TALK FOR INFORMATION AND
TALK FOR ACTION

One serious danger arises when two adults, let us say a mother and father, talk for action or for specific information with a child: contradiction. The child asks the parents what he should do, and Mother says he should do one thing while Father says that that is precisely what he should not do. When a child is given contradictory advice he is in a very sticky position. What does he do when that contradiction comes from the two main authorities in his life—his mother and father? I don't have an answer to the question, and more importantly, neither does the child.

Parents will disagree; they need not constantly present the face of perfect harmony to their children. The children will, for the most part, see beyond the facade anyway; if they don't, they will get a false picture of adult life. Even the most compatible of couples will have serious disagreements about important matters. But there are times when children need certain information, and there are times when children need to act within a given period of time. At those times, when we are talking for information or for a specific action, we should be very careful to avoid contradictory advice. We know, of course, that one person can give contradictory advice, but the more adults one allows into a conversation, the greater the chance that contradictory advice will be given and, subsequently, the greater the chance the child will be unable to act or to act well.

Another problem that often arises when adults talk with children is that the child is excluded from the conversation. Adults, as the more skilled language users, have a tendency to take conversations over. When skilled language users get together, they tend to talk to each other, and the unskilled child is often excluded from such conversations. This is troubling for children, and it should be troubling for those who are concerned about talking with children. It should be especially so when it occurs in talk for information or for a specific action. You should do whatever you can to counteract this tendency to monopolize. Ask yourself whether you are talking about the child's problems and giving the child sufficient time to talk about those problems. In order for your conversations to be successful there will have to be a good deal of agreement between or among the adults involved. If all the adults are not aware of the kind of conversation they are engaging in—if one thinks that they are talking for a specific action and the other thinks they are talking for discovery and invention—the talk will probably break down. Agreement, then, is crucial. Adults should spend some time before they talk with their children talking about *how* they will talk with their children.

TALK TO PASS THE TIME

Disagreements are not troublesome in talk for time-passing. Indeed, they often are essential to the game. They give us something to talk about. In the following conversation, Mother, Father, Ruth, and Paul are on their way to the beach. Paul is thirteen; Ruth is seven. The topic is the radio.

PAUL: Daddy, do we have to listen to that stuff every Saturday? The same dumb jokes about Lake Woebegone, wherever that is. . .

FATHER: It's in Minnesota. At least, that's what the announcer says.

PAUL: The same dumb jokes and the same old music.

FATHER: It's not the same. That's what is so good about it. You get old-time jazz singers, and folk music from the sixties, the odd Madrigal, a little ragtime. It's not just the same old stuff.

RUTH: No rock 'n' roll. No good music.

FATHER: No rock 'n' roll? Are you kidding? The Coasters were on last week. The Coasters are rock 'n' roll.

MOTHER: They might have been rock and roll to us. But they are not to the children. The children want to hear hard rock. AC/DC. Journey. Styx. The Coasters mean nothing to them.

RUTH: Yeah, tell him Mom.

MOTHER: Wait a minute. I agree with your Dad. I think the *Prairie Home Companion* is a wonderful show. Good, different music and a wonderful host. I think they just don't play much rock and roll that kids would like.

RUTH: Yeah, let's listen to some good rock 'n' roll—the kind kids would like.

PAUL: Yeah, give us kids a break.

FATHER: Ann, did you ever think this would happen? Remember when we first got married? How long ago that seems.

MOTHER: How long ago that was.

FATHER: Yeah, we thought things would be different with us and our kids. Our kids grew up listening to Bob Dylan and Joan Baez, the Beatles and the Rolling Stones, I never thought you could find *them* boring. Perry Como or Patti Page, O.K. But Bob Dylan or the Rolling Stones, never. Our kids groan when they hear us talk about Dylan just like we used to groan when our parents talked about Perry Como. Hard to believe, huh?

MOTHER: It sure is.

RUTH: Daddy, please put something else on.

MOTHER: Ruth, please be quiet. Daddy is feeling old. He is reminiscing.

RUTH: Mommy, stop talking funny. You always talk funny.

FATHER: Yeah, you always talk funny. I guess that's because you're getting old.

PAUL: You talk even funnier than Mommy. I guess that's because you're getting old.

FATHER: Please, no more old jokes.

MOTHER: Why don't we turn off the radio and just sing songs. That's what we used to do when I was a little girl.

FATHER: There's the sign for the turn-off for the bridge.

PAUL: Good. Then we don't have to sing songs.

RUTH: Or listen to that dumb show.

FATHER: Did your parents used to say to you when you did something that upset them, "Just wait till you have kids of your own"?

MOTHER: Sure, everybody's parents did that.

FATHER: I think I know what they meant now.

MOTHER: I know. Ruth, Paul, "Just wait till you have kids of your own."

RUTH: Oh, Mom!

PAUL: You're talking funny again.

MOTHER: I know. But it feels good.

This family is talking to pass some time. There are disagreements between the parents and some very low-level con-
flicts between parents and children. However, for the most
part, the style of all the talkers is light and bantering. The
conversation is not significant as such; no one expects to discover or invent anything. No one needs to perform a specific
action consequent to the conversation. No information is
needed. If the parents disagree or even if one parent has contradictory opinions—if, for example, the mother claimed to love
rock and roll but also claims to hate all rock and roll songs,
there is no need for the conversation to fail. Often, we switch
topics and pass the time by talking of different things; often we
are inconsistent.

If you pay a little attention to the preceding conversation,
you will note that at various times different speakers drop out.
This is typical of the genre, especially when groups of three or
more are speaking. There is nothing wrong with this. Sometimes, we just get bored with conversation and we drift off. At
other times, we have little to add so we just listen. The important thing for us, as parents, to remember is that when we are
talking for time-passing with our children, we should make it
just as easy for them to get back in the conversation after they
have left it as it was for them to exit from it in the first place.

TALK FOR DISCOVERY

One would think that the more people involved in an
attempt at discovery, the greater the chances of discovery.
When a conversation between a large number of adults and a
large number of children (or any combination of the two
groups) goes well, it is an exciting thing to see. But sadly
enough, one does not see it that often.

As in talk for time-passing, disagreements here are not
critical. Adults can disagree on what is important; they can
disagree on virtually everything. Children can handle all of
that when talking for discovery. What they cannot handle,
what none of us can handle, is the introduction of a whole

multitude of topics. In an ordinary talk for discovery a series of topics and subtopics are introduced. When things are going well, the change from one topic to another is almost organic; it seems natural to move from this topic to that. The move maintains the level of involvement for each speaker and leads to further discovery. This is what happens when the talk is going well. There is, however, a limit to the number of topics that can be introduced before the speakers become overwhelmed and lose interest. This can happen, of course, in any conversation. It is most apt to happen, however, in those conversations where more than two people are involved.

In the following conversation, a counselor, a teacher, and the seventh-grade student council representative, Jed, talk about, it would seem, almost everything. They are trying to decide how best to encourage students to have more school spirit.

COUNSELOR: Jed, it was very nice of you to stay after school and help Ms. Ziegler and I try to figure out what to do about school spirit. This is a new junior high school and no one seems to have any feelings for the school.

JED: Well . . .

TEACHER: New school. You are right; we may just have to wait for the school to build a tradition. Sometimes you just cannot rush things.

COUNSELOR: I am not trying to rush it. I just want to help it along. It is a great feeling for a kid to go to a school that he really cares about.

TEACHER: That *is* nice. Tradition and all that. But the primary purpose of school is for these kids—kids like Jed—to get an education, to learn about important subjects like math and English and civics.

JED: Mr. Snider, I thought you wanted to talk about school spirit. How come we're talking about math and all that stuff?

COUNSELOR: Ms. Ziegler has a very good point. Sometimes we have to talk about things—about other things—before we can talk about what we may want to talk about. It's like this. You cannot just go right on and do algebra. You have to learn other things first. You have to, for example, learn something about arithmetic before you can move on to algebra.

TEACHER: Thank you, Mr. Snider. That is a very important lesson for a young boy to learn. That is the problem with children today. They want the answers but they are not willing to do the work necessary to arrive at those answers. If they cannot get their answer right away, they just seem to lose interest.

COUNSELOR: But, don't you think that that is the way it has always been? Or, at least, the way it was when we were young?

TEACHER: You have a point. Sometimes, as adults, we tend to forget what it was like when we were young. That is an important point for us to remember. *(Pause)* I just learned something. And let me point something out to you, young man, that I wouldn't have learned that—or been reminded of it—if we had just hurried to get the answer to our little problem. I hope you have learned something, too.

JED: I did, Ms. Ziegler. It's just that I'm supposed to meet some of the kids in the gym. We were going to shoot some baskets.

COUNSELOR: Do you think that that is more important than helping your school and your classmates?

JED: *(Pause)* No, sir. But that's why I came here. To talk about school spirit. Ms. O'Brien asked me to come because, I guess, she thought I was a good student and I had school spirit, and she wanted me to help you. That's why I came.

TEACHER: Good. And that is why we want you here, to represent your peers and to tell us what we might do to improve school spirit.

COUNSELOR: Where is Ms. O'Brien? It's a shame she couldn't be with us.

TEACHER: Maybe we could have her present at our next meeting. Will you be free after school tomorrow, Jed?

JED: Yes, Ma'am.

The obvious problem here is that a series of diverse topics are inserted into the conversation, and Jed cannot see the connection among them. As the conversation moves away from what he is interested in, he becomes increasingly lost and disinterested. Jed, we may assume, is discovering nothing new, and most importantly, he is not being *encouraged* to discover anything new.

Besides flip-flopping from one topic to another, the teacher and the counselor make two crucial mistakes. First, sensing that Jed is losing interest in the conversation, they attempt to shame him into taking part. In effect, they attempt to shame him into discovery. In principle, this sort of technique may work in the odd case; however, it is generally a sure-fire way to ensure that the child will lose interest in the topics to be discussed. Second, and this may be the most reprehensible thing adults can do when talking for discovery with children, they gang-up on Jed. Adults, as we have said, are more sophisticated language users than children. In an argument between adults and children, children typically lose. Jed would not be able to hold his own with one adult; with two well-educated adults, he is forced either to agree or to remain silent.

TALK FOR SHARING

We might with profit appropriate here a term from sociology. That term is "cohort." Your cohort is somebody who grew up at approximately the same time as you and who had similar experiences at approximately the same times. If there are any absolutes, here is one. When our cohort speaks about his feelings, especially when he talks about his past, we tend to pay attention and we tend to find what he says interesting. When you meet someone of approximately your age, you generally find yourself, in some sense, drawn to her. You probably will want to exchange stories and histories with her, and will be very interested to find out how she survived the hard times you survived, what she thinks about them now, and what she thinks about the present time. The simple cohort relationship may be enough to engender a very rich talk for sharing. Now, the simple fact is that you and your child can never be cohorts. You can never share memories in the same way that you would with an old college roommate. This does not mean, of course, that you cannot share memories with your child or that these memories cannot be of major significance. It means, simply, that given your respective ages, you and your child are precluded from enjoying one sort of relationship, that of cohorts.

There is something else that cohorts are prone to do; they tend to talk in a kind of shorthand. Cohorts know what is to be assumed; there is no need for them to go through the step-by-step, rather laborious process of uncovering and labeling assumptions. Linguistically, they can move so quickly that their conversation is nearly incomprehensible to an outsider. Listen to the talk of two jazz musicians of approximately the same age, and you will know exactly what I mean. Finally, cohorts tend to utilize the same connotation systems. If you grew up during the Depression, a term like "poverty" will mean something quite different for you and your cohorts from what it means to those raised in a more affluent time.

When one adult talks with one child, the adult is more likely to speak to a shared interest, to avoid shorthand, and to utilize connotations the child will comprehend. When another adult enters the conversation, especially if the other adult is a cohort of the first, the balance is shifted. The adults become less likely to speak to an interest that they and the child share. They become less likely to avoid shorthand, and they become less likely to utilize connotations they share with the child. In short, the more adults that enter the conversation, the greater the chance that the child will be left out. This does not always happen, and it is not sufficient reason to exclude other adults from your talks for sharing. But these are real dangers to talking with your children. There may be no sure-fire way to avoid them, but simple awareness of their existence is often enough. You must repeatedly ask yourself whether you are sharing something with *all* the other talkers—cohorts and children—and whether they are, in turn, sharing with you. If not, then you have a problem that you should take steps to correct.

One last point is appropriate. Sometimes we talk with more than one child, and children, of course, can be cohorts, too. As cohorts, they can do the same things, fall into the same traps, adults do. Children, just like adults, have a right to talk among themselves. They have a right to their own experiences, their own shorthand, and their own connotations. However, when they talk with adults some common ground is needed. Adults have greater linguistic power than children and may be a good deal more able to translate the speech of child-cohorts so that the talk for sharing can proceed effectively. Still, the linguistic power of adults is not unlimited. Sometimes, they, too, may be left out of conversations because they are not cohorts of the other speakers. At this point, it seems to me, adults have a right to demand that assumptions be marked, that shorthand speech be dropped, and so on. If the children are not willing or are not able to do that, then there is little reason to continue with the conversation. It would be better to allow the child-cohorts their own conversations and to talk with them later when they are ready for or when they are desirous of talking for sharing with adults. Just as you cannot force someone to love or feel pity or be fond of something, you cannot force children to talk for sharing. You simply have to wait until they are ready.

TALKING
AND
THE SCHOOLS

It is very easy to take potshots at the schools. They present a ridiculously easy target to hit. "The schools are not working. Children do not seem to know as much as they used to. They do not seem to be as well-prepared as they used to be. Their scores on standardized tests are going down. Children graduate from high school and still cannot read or do basic mathematics."

But it is even easier to take potshots at parents. "Sure, schools are bad, but they are bad because parents have not prepared their children for schools. Nowadays (whenever you see "nowadays," it is safe to assume that a severe criticism will follow), parents are too busy with their own lives to take the time to be with their children, to discipline them and give them the love and attention they need. Parents bundle their kids off to day-care centers (it is also very easy to take potshots at day-care centers) and the children are raised in a cold, sterile environment where no one takes a personal, sustained interest in their development."

Many, though perhaps not all of these criticisms are overstated and unfair. It is extremely difficult to raise children and to educate them. Indeed, it is amazing that parents and schools do as well as they do. My intention here is not to rake the schools over some familiar coals, but to point to the need for some sort of continuum between the school and the home as talking environments. View the following as gentle suggestions to parents and to teachers.

HOW TO CONFUSE A CHILD COMPLETELY

Picture the following extreme situation. Roger is five years old. His parents have read this book, they liked what was in it and, since Roger has been speaking, have engaged him in the various kinds of talk mentioned here. They have encouraged him to express his opinions and to give the best reasons possible for those opinions. In short, they have encouraged talking and thinking. Simply, Roger, little five-year-old Roger, is the sort of child who talks and thinks a lot and who values those activities. This does not mean, of course, that Roger does not value listening and does not know that there are times when silence is appropriate. *Indeed, if he is a good talker, he is a good listener.* But there are times when Roger *wants* to talk, when he wants to contribute to the conversation.

In September Roger is sent off to school. Roger learns, in this extreme situation, that he must not talk. He learns that his talking is considered an interruption unless he is responding to a question from his teacher. When he talks to his neighbor he is considered a behavioral problem. He gets a "U" on his report card under the category "conduct." When he talks out of turn to his teacher, he is considered a discipline problem. When he talks to the teacher, but gives the wrong answer, he is accused either of being stupid or of not having done his homework. In effect, Roger is being told that only one kind of talk is important in the classroom: a very truncated version of what we have called talk for information. All other kinds of talk—talk for discovery, talk for sharing, talk for a specific action, talk for time-passing—are inappropriate to the classroom. The kinds of talk that are interesting and important to him, the talks that occupy most of his time, have no place in the classroom.

This, it would seem, would be very confusing to young Roger. He has the two greatest authorities in his life—parent and teacher—sending him contradictory messages. His parents have shown him that his active involvement in talk is both necessary and good. His teacher has made clear that Roger's active involvement in talk (Roger's actual speaking) is neither necessary nor good. Not a bad way to confuse a child. But we can point to some ways to avoid the problem.

We might suggest that Roger be told that the school and the home are markedly different environments, and that what is appropriate behavior in one will be inappropriate in the other. In school, we absorb information. We do this best by listening, taking notes, and responding to explicit questions asked by the teacher. At home, we try to discover and invent. We try to share feelings. We pass the time. We try to do different things, things we do best by talking. We can say those things to Roger and we will help him to avoid certain confusions. He will be able to say that talking is best here (in the home) but is not best there (in the school).

Another way we might help Roger over his confusion is by removing one of the sources of the confusion. To oversimplify, it would appear that his parents believe talk for discovery to be a good thing and that his teachers disagree. His parents, then, could modify their stance. They could say that talk for discovery is not a good thing. That is one way, one pretty miserable way, of avoiding the confusion.

On the other hand, his teachers, in this extreme situation, might modify their position. They might say that talk for discovery is a good thing. This would put them in agreement with the parents and would remove the cause of Roger's confusion. It would, however, cause those teachers, in that extreme situation, radically to overhaul the way they teach. It would cause their school to look quite different from what it originally appeared to be.

We might also suggest, as a means of avoiding the confusion, that Roger not have to deal with both environments. Simply, the parents could refuse to allow children to go to school or the teachers could refuse to allow Roger to go home.

WHAT A SCHOOL IS

A school, for the most part, is a simplified learning environment. In an earlier time, children could learn everything they needed to know in the home or in the neighborhood or by being apprenticed to some expert. The child could pick up everything he needed to know simply by existing in the environment in which he found himself. He got all his important information at his father's knee.

That kind of education, call it informal education, was sufficient in a time when society was relatively simple. It was sufficient when parents knew all that the children had to know and when the parents knew how to convey all that the children had to know. Today, given the complexity of our world, parents simply do not have the expertise to convey to children all that they will need to know when they become adults.

The task of the school—at least, a primary task of the school—is to simplify things so that children learn what will help them make their way in the world. Some of the things the child has to know are facts—bits of information—and sometimes, the child must simply be told those things. (I am not arguing, then, against truncated talks for information; it seems to me that there is a real place for that—especially in the schools.)

But other things that the child needs to know cannot simply be dictated to her. Our world is changing rapidly. We do not know what a child will need to know in 20 years. The most we can do is to try to help her to develop the skills that will enable her to deal with her environment, whatever that environment may turn out to be. These skills we might call thinking skills—skills that enable a child to deal with that which is presented to her.

Now, the question remains how the schools can best aid the child in developing thinking skills. I have opinions on this and I am sure you can guess what they are, but here I will assert only that talking with the child is one of the best ways and that if you only talk with a child for information you will not do much to help develop his thinking skills. Talk for information may provide him with a great many facts, but unless he can put those facts together, unless he can see the connections among them, his knowledge will not be of much use to him. What you have to do, as I have spent a whole book suggesting, is talk for discovery, talk for sharing feelings, and so on. Do that and you will begin to have some impact on your child's thinking skills.

Since the school is or should be desirous of having an impact on thinking skills, it should encourage the same sorts of activities—talking activities—that you perform with your child. Teachers *should* talk for discovery with children. This does not mean that parent-child talk should be identical to teacher-student talk. Obviously, there will be differences. But even given the constraints imposed upon teachers by the curriculum and by time we can ask that teachers take some time to engage in talk other than talk for information. Otherwise the chances that they will have a positive impact on the student's thinking skills are slim.

Let me repeat, most schools and most educators are aware of the fact that children need the opportunity to talk. Most schools and most educators do not treat, or, at least, do not want to treat children as if they were mindless tape recorders. However, the press of the curriculum would seem to *require* a very truncated version of talk for information. As more information is added to the curriculum, as the curriculum expands, teachers find themselves spending more and more time on talk for information. As a result, the other kinds of talk are neglected and the ordinary class becomes dangerously close to the extreme one in which Roger found himself.

Since we do not want ourselves and our children (and our teachers) to be in that extreme situation, it is incumbent on us to do whatever is in our power to decrease the likelihood that the situation will occur. This means that, at the very least, parents should let educators—specifically, boards of education—know that they value not only talk for information, but all the other kinds of talk as essential to the primary task of the school: helping children to develop their thinking skills so that they might better cope with their environment.

One might hear at this point the beleaguered voice of the school teacher: "You tell me that there are a certain number of facts that I must get across to my students. Fine, I can do that. I will talk for information with them. Then you tell me I must attempt to develop their thinking skills. But since talk for information only gives them facts and does not show them how to use those facts, I discover that I must encourage the children in other kinds of talk. Fine, again. You have made my task much harder. At times I will be overwhelmed, but still you have given me a task which, if I am extremely conscientious, I can successfully complete. Now you do something else. You look around the world and you notice important subjects that are not in the curriculum. You want me to give information about sex and drugs and citizenship. Well, I can't do all that talk for information and still talk in the other ways with the children. There simply is not enough time."

This teacher is not talking nonsense. The "stuff" of the curriculum has expanded a great deal in the last few decades. Many teachers today find themselves in a position where they simply do not have the time to let children talk for discovery, to let them try to figure things out for themselves. Since we, as parents, are concerned about this and since we do want the teachers to have the time to talk with our children (to talk in ways other than talk for information), we have an obligation to begin thinking about what should go in the curriculum and what should not. It is recognized now that there is too much in the curriculum. The curriculum is too crowded; something will have to come out. But what? Some will say that the only thing the school should do is deal with the traditional 3 Rs. Others argue that only those subjects should be taught that directly prepare the children for adulthood. Still others, that education should prepare the child only to be a moral, responsible citizen. And finally, there are those who say that all subjects which contribute to the child's total development should be taught.

Difficulties arise with all of these. I have my opinions as to the best alternative (it is not listed above), but it would take me another book to give my reasons. The only thing I am saying here is that you should *begin* thinking or you should think *more* about the problem of the curriculum. If there is a solution—and it strikes me that assuming there is not only breeds despair—the chances of our finding it without talking or thinking about it are slim. Although *your* thinking and talking may not solve the problem, it might contribute to the solution. It might encourage others to take the problem seriously.

That is what *you* should do. But, as educators always say, the education of the child involves a kind of partnership between home and school. There must, then, be something that educators should do. More precisely, there are some *things* that educators should do. First, they should refrain from throwing up their hands and saying nothing can be done to solve the problem. Second, they should begin to think about the problem again; they should try different ways of attacking it. Third, they should recognize that the problem is, in part, a function of overcrowding the curriculum. That last point could stand a little development. Look at this example. A second-grade teacher is given six hours in the day. Two hours are given over to recreation, lunch, moving from classroom to classroom, and so on. That leaves four hours. During those four hours, the teacher must devote two hours to mathematics, one hour to social studies, and one to language arts. In language arts, she must devote one half hour to reading. She is pressed for time; she has little opportunity to *discuss* anything with the children. What can the educator do to help her? How can he give her more time? The obvious thing would be to delete one subject. Eliminate math, for example, and you pick up an additional two hours—plenty of time for talk for discovery. But the educator cannot do this because, we may assume, he has not arrived at adequate criteria for saying what should and what should not go in the curriculum. Why should he take out mathematics and not, say, language arts? Why not social studies?

Still, there is something that the educator can do. He can use whatever expertise he has to make sure that the subjects are being taught as efficiently as possible. He can determine whether the talk for information is as economical as possible. In order to help that second-grade teacher, and all other teachers, the educator might review the entire curriculum, not with an eye to removing things, but simply with the intention of ensuring that information be presented when children are most receptive to it and when they are best able to handle it. He might find, for example, that reading instruction for children should begin a great deal later than it does in our public schools. It might turn out that if we introduce children to reading in the fifth grade, they may arrive at a tenth grade reading level in five years. It now, typically, takes us ten years to achieve that level. I am not saying that this would be the case; I am only illustrating here a *method,* but if the educators did discover that, they would have come up with a means of giving the teacher a good deal more time to talk with her students.

But we must keep in mind that schools are not automated factories; we must maintain our standards for success and failure, standards which recognize that each student is unique. To underscore what I mean, let me bend, if not completely break our rule against making universal statements and our rule against talking about human nature. People need to talk. Take talking away from them and you deprive them of something valuable. Take talking away from them when they are children and the process of education grinds to a halt. We must make a space—a large space—in the curriculum where the need of a child to talk is recognized and encouraged. In order to make that space, we may appear to be fanatical about efficiency and economy. But if we are, it is only in order that the child can have time in the course of her day to be inefficient and uneconomical—time to talk for discovery, to talk for sharing some feeling, and so on.

We have just placed a burden on the educator. We have asked him to rearrange the curriculum. Historically, when similar burdens were placed on the educator, he would simply pick up a book on developmental psychology, look for the ages when children were capable of performing particular activities, and then make sure that at the appropriate age the child would be studying the appropriate subjects. Thus, educators discovered such things as "reading readiness"; they found that it is a mistake to try to teach someone to read before he or she is ready for it.

Developmental psychology has been an invaluable tool for the contemporary educator, and, in many respects, it has humanized the classroom. We no longer berate the first grader who cannot read. But there are a few traps that educators might fall into when they use the findings of developmental psychology to decide curricular matters, traps that educators and all the rest of us may fall into whenever we use science to deal with educational problems.

DEVELOPMENTAL PSYCHOLOGY AS A FINISHED PRODUCT

The ordinary person, you or I, tends to view science as being composed of a set of propositions that are either true or false—the earth is not flat; water is denser than air—and that the scientist is the person who can differentiate between the two. But one does not "know" a science when one can recognize the true propositions. A science is an activity that involves using the true propositions and the more theoretical propositions (propositions that have not been shown to be true) in order to explain, to predict, and to attempt control.

Developmental psychology is a science like any other. It is an instrument to be used with a good deal of caution. But in comparison with the other sciences, developmental psychology is still in its infancy. There is, and there should be, a kind of tentativeness in its propositions. To use the findings of developmental psychology as a sourcebook or as a starting point seems good sense; to use the findings of developmental psychology as the final word on the subject is to misunderstand the nature of the science. Just as politicians can use the findings of physics to build bombs that explode efficiently (kill a lot of people and destroy a lot of property), to build bombs that do not explode efficiently (only kill some people; only damage some property) or to increase our energy resources, so educators can use the findings of developmental psychology to paralyze children emotionally and cognitively, to paralyze them partially or to increase their cognitive and emotional mobility.

THE LITERAL INTERPRETATION OF DEVELOPMENTAL PSYCHOLOGY

One of the most important names in developmental psychology is Jean Piaget. Piaget and his followers have done a great deal of work with children over the last 40 years. One of his findings is that children, all children, seem to go through a four-stage process of development. At stage one, the child will be able to perform some but not other cognitive activities. It is only at the fourth stage, the stage Piaget called the "formal-operational" stage, that children can perform all the cognitive activities that a typical adult can perform. Therefore, for example, it is a mistake to try to teach a child something about deductive logic before the child is at the formal-operational stage. That child simply does not have the appropriate cognitive structures to deal with that material.

But Piaget did not intend educators to take his findings literally. He published his work as the findings of research done over specific populations during specific periods of time. He said, for example, that the children he studied typically reached the formal-operational stage at around 11 years. We have no reason to believe that Piaget believed that children *must* reach given stages at given ages or that cultural differences might not affect the development of children. Indeed, Piaget, like all good scientists, is very slow to generalize, and when he does generalize, he does so only with a good number of qualifying remarks.

Being in research, Piaget did not have to reach a conclusion until the evidence warranted it. Educators, on the other hand, are pressed for time. They must act. They must design a curriculum. And in their haste, they may simply appropriate the findings of Piaget and other developmental psychologists in ways that would appall reputable psychologists.

DEVELOPMENTAL PSYCHOLOGY AS THE ONLY SOURCE OF INFORMATION

In the twentieth century, the best tool that we have for explanation, prediction, and control is science. In the twentieth century, the best tool that we have for explanation, prediction, and control of the activities of children is developmental psychology. This does not mean, however, that the methods of developmental psychology are the only methods that we might use with profit to come to an understanding of childhood or, in general, that developmental psychology is our only important source for knowledge about children. As any reputable developmental psychologist will tell you, there are other sources. Let me list just a few.

Reports of Experienced People. Experience gives no guarantee. Quite often, we learn nothing of value from our experiences. However, there are times when we do learn valuable lessons that we can apply to subsequent experiences. Now, these people with the most experience are typically older people. The reports of these people—our parents and grandparents—should be taken, it seems to me, in the same way that we take the reports of developmental psychologists. They should be taken as evidence that we can use when we make our decisions about children.

The Reports of Poets and Novelists. Poets and novelists spend a great deal of time talking about what it is like to be a child. We would all be well advised to read Walt Whitman or E. B. White and to take their statements and the statements of similar writers into account when we make our decisions about children. Ignoring *Tom Sawyer,* it seems to me, is equivalent to ignoring Jean Piaget. Ignore either and your task is made harder than it might be.

The Experience That We Have with Our Children. Developmental psychologists can tell us important things about types of children and about what we might expect typical children to do in typical situations. Our parents and grandparents can tell us about their children and how they dealt with them. Poets and novelists can tell us about the characters they have created, the characters they remember being. We, in turn, can use all of that information when we deal with our children. But there are significant differences between our children and all other children. There is information about our children that only we who live with them and talk with them can know. In a very real sense, we are the experts about our own children. Talk with your children. Do not just adopt what you have read, but *adapt* it to them.